On Foot in North Lesvos

by Mike Maunder

The Olive Press

First published as 'Mithimna Walks' March 2000
Reprinted with minor revisions May 2000
Revised and enlarged edition
'On Foot in North Lesvos'
published January 2001
Reprinted April, June 2001, January, June 2002

This further enlarged and fully revised edition
first published January 2003

ISBN 0-9539214-3-3

Published at
The Olive Press'
by M Maunder
R6 Marine Gate, Marine Drive
Brighton BN2 5TN, UK
email: lesvos_walks@yahoo.co.uk
phone +44 (0)1273 675434

On Foot in North Lesvos
Update 2006

This leaflet covers changes on the ground between October 2002 and October 2005, plus a few corrections and clarifications to the original text. It replaces the printed leaflet 'Update 2005' and 'Stop Press 2005' on www.lesvoswalks.net

General: New green fingerposts, apparently intended for walkers, have appeared at track junctions throughout Lesvos. As well as the obvious places, Eftalou, Argenos, etc., a number point down tracks I know to be dead ends, and to places (probably shrines or farms) unfamiliar to me and others I have spoken to.

Walk 3, page 8: There are new signs to the horse track (ΠΡΟΣ ΙΠΠΟΔΡΟΜΟ), with white lettering on a blue background, at the beginning of the walk by the farmers' co-operative olive factory, and at junctions along the way.

Walk 5, page 11, para 4: The track has now been extended into the valley. Follow it downhill from the beginning until it levels out (about 2 mins). The path forks off left at this point.
Page 12, para 4: There may be a brushwood barrier at the olive grove boundary with the river bank.

Walk 6: page 14, para 3: The "Building Land For Sale" board has been replaced by one reading "PANORAMA".
A large new house has been built around the chapel; several other new houses are going up on plots to the right of the path.

Walk 7, page 16, para 5: This track has been widened and graded throughout most of its length to Petra. It may be about to be upgraded to a tarmac road.

Walk 8, page 20, line 1: The word 'right' could be misleading: the path drops down to the right of the main track, but bears left where it leaves the track.
Para 4: The brushwood gate has been removed. Go through the remaining gate and bear right into the field.

Walk 9, page 23, para 1: A new track has been driven up the lower part of the hillside, starting about 20 metres downstream from the previous crossing. (It is clearly visible across the valley as you walk down towards the farm) To reach it, go between the farm buildings and the stream and continue across the farmyard. Follow the track up the hill, ignoring the branch to the left running along the hillside.

The track currently ends at the first ridge, where a field has been fenced. At the brow of the hill there is a row of small trees to the left - take the path that runs alongside and immediately before them.
Most of the water pipe has now been removed.
Para 5: 10 metres beyond the gate a rough track has now been bulldozed down to meet the top of the existing track.
page 23, last para: The goat path has disappeared. It is now easier to walk diagonally across to the top right-hand corner of the range and climb the barbed wire fence in the corner of the field where piled stones form a stile. Then follow the path to the right through the brushwood fence and left downhill.

Walk 10, page 25, para 3: Shortly below the beginning of the path a new track has been bulldozed, obliterating a section. Turn left on to the track (this is the second track, the first runs down to a metal gate), follow round the right-hand bend and climb for 5 minutes until a short spur joins acutely from the right. The path resumes a few metres down here on the left. I have added new blue way marks on this section.

Walk 11, page 26, Introduction: I understand that Fr Ignatius is no longer at Ypsilometopo. I do not know whether his replacement is continuing his custom of welcoming visitors.

Page 30, para 1: Halfway down the hill there is a new dirt road off to the left (signposted KAΛΛONH) This runs along the hillside above Stipsi and leads to the junction in Walk 16, page 41, para 2.

Walk 12, page 31, para 3: Shortly after the second gate there is a new track down to the right: keep on the upper track.

Para 4: There are new blue way marks from the first mill as far as page 33, para 1.

Page 32, para 2: The gate has been removed.

Paras 2-3: There seems to have been some confusion here: to clarify, the path leads uphill to the left immediately before (ie to the left of) the cistern.

Last para: This post and the way marks have now completely disappeared. For Petri take the path down into the valley starting to the left of the large triangular outcrop in the shape of a shark's fin.

Page 33, para 1: This tree becomes lower each year. Bend double to pass and notice the remains of another mill which were previously hidden behind its branches.
Immediately after this, by a fallen tree with a blue circle mark (the last of the new marks) you may notice a small way mark and blue arrow below on the opposite side of the valley. Ignore this.

Para 4: Shortly after the brushwood barrier (which if you stay in the stream-bed can now be walked under without difficulty) the stream divides. Follow the right-hand channel (previously this was the obvious route, but it has been obscured by fallen trees) or for easier walking climb on to its left-hand bank. Almost immediately go through a gap in a wall towards the animal shed. (If you come across a much larger shed surrounded by a network of wiremesh fences you have followed the wrong channel)

Walk 13, page 34, para 2: Shortly after the second gate there is a new track down to the right. Both tracks lead to the chapel.

Para 4: The grassy track has been widened, and is no longer grassy. Now, where you meet the kalderimi leading ahead, bear left slightly uphill through a gate.

Walk 14, page 36, para 3: The Grand Café has now closed and its sign has been removed.

Page 36, para 3, last sentence: A large new house is being built on the left behind a high stone wall. There may be some builders' rubble on the path.

NB: Someone has added large waymark arrows in red paint on the upper sections of this walk. They are nothing to do with me and seem to relate to a different route.

Page 37, para 1: After rejoining the Petra-Petri road, in order to avoid following it up past the rubbish tip, turn left after about 50 metres up a steep concrete drive. This becomes a track leading up to a new house behind steel gates on the left. Go on to the stone wall ahead, then left up a faint path. This winds uphill, partly on old kalderimi, and comes out at the new apartment block. Turn left to follow the track up to the church.

Park on H
J & M

Mike Maunder, R6 Marine Gate, Marine Drive, Brighton BN2 5TN, UK
Phone +44 (0) 1273 675434   Mobile (UK) +44 (0) 778 6242179 (Greece) +30 694 5819546
www.lesvoswalks.net   email: mike@lesvoswalks.net

On Foot in North Lesvos

**As promised, here is 'Update 2006' for insertion in your book. Please
discard the 'Update 2005' insert, which it replaces.**

Mike Maunder

16/11/2005

With Compliments

The Olive Press

Walk 15: page 39, para 2: Be sure to continue on the path downhill as far as the stream. Ignore any waymarks indicating a path to the right.

Walk 16, page 41, para 1: Harald Haugli, a reader who has done this walk with an altimeter, tells me that this is not the summit of Roussa, which in fact is about 83m (270') higher and 1km further east. His instructions to get there (which I have not yet tried) are:- "It is easy to get there, there are plenty of animal tracks going in the right direction and a concrete post marks the summit. Curve back above the main antenna using what you can find. Then go through a gate in the stone wall to your right. After that it is just to aim for the top of the hill (or the post if you can spot it), keeping the wall fairly close on your left where the animal tracks are easiest for walking"

Walk 17, page 43, first line: A new hand-painted sign to Eftalou has appeared, pointing right through a gap in the wall on to the drive from the new development. Following this will lead you on to the track past the Pension Taverna Orpheus (page 44, para 4). If you want to follow the coastline, stay with the instructions in the book.

Walk 18, page 46, para 2: The millstones have gone.

Walk 20: page 50, para 2: Take care not to miss this right turn; the bottom of the track is becoming overgrown. It is opposite the steel/wire mesh gate of a fenced olive grove.
Para 3: Immediately before the first house on the left a short track has been bulldozed up to the left. This leads directly to the square, next to the school, with the Taverna ΤΟ ΑΙΘΡΙΟΝ immediately to the right, making a useful short cut if you are desperate for a beer after the climb.

Walk 21, page 51, para 2, line 10: For a short cut avoiding most of the bypass; about five minutes along the lane there is a staggered crossroad with signs to 'Center' and 'Anaxos'. Turn left here, walk up to the bypass and turn right. The track to Lafionas is about 40m on the left, just after a large new pale blue agricultural building.
Para 3: A new track has been opened up into an olive grove. Coming from Anaxos the track to Lafionas is now the third on the right.
Page 52, last para: There is a large new water-trough shortly before the junction.

Walk 22, page 53, para 3: The first sentence should read: 'Take the left-hand street out of the square into the village, and almost immediately the first turning on the left. Follow it as it bends round to the right.....'
The sign on the electricity pole has disappeared (there are various new signs around the village indicating the 'road' route to Ag. Alexandros) Several of the way marks have faded into near invisibility, but the path remains clear.
Page 54, para 2: The fountain has now been removed.
Para 3: Ignore the new track forking down to the right just after the monastery, unless you want an extra ten minute walk to a promontory with views over towards Skoutaros.

(For a new route through the valley to the Skoutaros-Anaxos road see my website)

Walk 23, page 56, para 3: The foot of the first uphill track has washed out and is easily missed; the second is almost at the brow of the hill near the seat.
Para 5, line 1: There is new sign here to Λαφιώνα - Lafiona.
The sign at the next fork has been corrected with a taped arrow pointing right to Ag Alexandros.

Walk 26: page 61, para 3: Beyond the waymark the path has been widened into a rough track (an extension of the one at the foot of the page, which now winds down from side to side of the valley) After a few minutes it bends right across the stream and doubles back uphill. The original path continues ahead on the left-hand side of the stream.

Para 5: The new track crosses the path again at this point, between the two giant trees. Follow it up to the left and sharply round to the right. At the next left-hand bend the Turkish fountain is on the right. Then continue from the top of page 62.

Page 62, para 4: The gate and warning signs at the top of the track have been removed - there is now no obstacle to getting to the summit of Vigla. The communications post looks abandoned, though there are still radio sets in place and the door remains locked.

Page 63, last line: Add 'In five minutes turn left again at another T'

Page 64, paras 2-4: New brushwood barriers have made it necessary to reroute this section, as follows: 'The path leads back into trees and descends again. It bends round to the right and climbs on kalderimi. Go through a gate and bear left, with the entrance to an olive grove straight ahead. Climb steeply over a brow and down again with a wall on the right. In five minutes, continue ahead onto an overgrown path along a terrace wall. After two minutes bear right past a fallen tree and continue along the path with steep terracing down on the right towards the sea.

In another five minutes, by an entrance on the left over a fallen wall into an olive grove, go straight ahead along an overgrown kalderimi running between walls. Bear right and continue slightly uphill. Go along the path as it reverts to kalderimi leading down and across a stream, then bending right under a high stone wall on the other side. (This last section has become very overgrown) It finally bends left and climbs twenty metres to join a dirt road by a small trekking trail sign'

Page 66, last para: The previous top of the path and part of the fence has been washed away. Now leave the road immediately after the right-hand bend as the trekking trail sign comes into view.

The next printed update will be produced in early 2007. For a free copy send an addressed envelope to the address below.

If you come across anything that you think should be noted, please let me know by email or letter.

For interim updates, additional routes, & more about Lesvos visit my website
www.lesvoswalks.net

The Olive Press

Published in January 2006 at:
The Olive Press
by M Maunder
R6 Marine Gate, Marine Drive
Brighton BN2 5TN, UK
email: mike@lesvoswalks.net
phone +44 (0)1273 675434

On Foot in North Lesvos
Update 2005

This leaflet covers changes on the ground between October 2002 and October 2004, plus a few corrections and clarifications to the original text. It replaces the printed leaflet 'Update 2004' and 'Stop Press 2004' on www.lesvoswalks.net

General: New green fingerposts, apparently intended for walkers, have appeared at track junctions throughout Lesvos. As well as the obvious places, Eftalou, Argenos, etc., a number point down tracks I know to be dead ends, and to places (probably shrines or farms) unfamiliar to me and others I have spoken to.

Walk 3, page 8: There are new signs to the horse track (ΠΡΟΣ ΙΠΠΟΔΡΟΜΟ), with white lettering on a blue background, at the beginning of the walk by the farmers' co-operative olive factory, and at junctions along the way.

Walk 5, page 11, para 4: The track has now been extended into the valley. Follow it downhill from the beginning until it levels out (about 2 mins). The path forks off left at this point.
Page 12, para 4: There may be a brushwood barrier at the olive grove boundary with the river bank.

Walk 6: page 14, para 3: A new house is being built around the chapel; three or four other new houses are going up on plots to the right of the path.
Page 15, para 1: There is a new gate just before the main entrance to Karuna. The gate at the foot of the uphill track, which had been removed, has now been replaced with a length of concrete reinforcing mesh.
Para 3: This gate has been removed and the track widened - look out for the right turn where the widened track continues ahead.

Walk 8, page 20, line 1: The word 'right' could be misleading: the path drops down to the right of the main track, but bears left where it leaves the track.
Para 4: The brushwood gate has been removed. Go through the remaining gate and bear right into the field.

Walk 9, page 23, para 1: The water pipe has now been removed.
Para 5: 10 metres beyond the gate a rough track has now been bulldozed down to meet the top of the existing track.
Last para: The barbed wire fence has to be climbed in the corner of the field where piled stones form a stile; then follow the path to the right through the gap in the brushwood fence and left downhill.

Walk 10, page 25, para 3: Shortly below the beginning of the path a new track has been bulldozed, obliterating a section. Turn left on to the track (this is the second track, the first runs down to a metal gate), follow round the right-hand bend and climb for 5 minutes until a short spur joins acutely from the right. The path resumes a few metres down here on the left. I have added new blue way marks on this section.

Walk 11, page 26, Introduction: I understand that Fr Ignatius is no longer at Ypsilometopo. I do not know whether his replacement is continuing his custom of welcoming visitors.

Page 30, para 1: Halfway down the hill there is a new dirt road off to the left (signposted ΚΑΛΛΟΝΗ) This runs along the hillside above Stipsi and leads to the junction in Walk 16, page 41, para 2.

Walk 12, page 31, para 3: Shortly after the second gate there is a new track down to the right: keep on the upper track.

Para 4: There are new blue way marks from the first mill as far as page 33, para 1.

Page 32, para 2: The gate has been removed.

Last para: These way marks have now almost completely disappeared. For Petri take the path down into the valley starting to the left of the large triangular outcrop in the shape of a shark's fin.

Page 33, para 1: This tree becomes lower each year. Bend double to pass and notice the remains of another mill which were previously hidden behind its branches.
Immediately after this, by a fallen tree with a blue circle mark (the last of the new marks) you may notice a small way mark and blue arrow below on the opposite side of the valley. Ignore this.

Walk 13, page 34, para 2: Shortly after the second gate there is a new track down to the right. Both tracks lead to the chapel.

Para 4: The grassy track has been widened, the gates removed, and is no longer grassy. Now, where you meet the kalderimi leading ahead, bear left slightly uphill.

Walk 14, page 36, para 3: The Grand Café has now closed and its sign has been removed.

Page 37, para 1: After rejoining the Petra-Petri road, in order to avoid following it up past the rubbish tip, turn left after about 50 metres up a steep concrete drive. This becomes a track leading up to a new house behind steel gates on the left. Go on to the stone wall ahead, then left up a faint path. This winds uphill, partly on old kalderimi, and comes out at the new apartment block. Turn left to follow the track up to the church.

Walk 15: page 39, para 2: Be sure to continue on the path downhill as far as the stream. Ignore any waymarks indicating a path to the right.

Walk 16, page 41, para 1: Harald Haugli, a reader who has done this walk with an altimeter, tells me that this is not the summit of Roussa, which in fact is about 83m (270') higher and 1km further east. His instructions to get there (which I have not yet tried) are:-
"It is easy to get there, there are plenty of animal tracks going in the right direction and a concrete post marks the summit. Curve back above the main antenna using what you can find. Then go through a gate in the stone wall to your right. After that it is just to aim for the top of the hill (or the post if you can spot it), keeping the wall fairly close on your left where the animal tracks are easiest for walking"

Walk 18, page 46, para 2: The millstones have gone.

Walk 20: page 50, para 3: Immediately before the first house on the left a short track has been bulldozed up to the left. This leads directly to the square, next to the school, with the Taverna TO ΑΙΘΡΙΟΝ immediately to the right, making a useful short cut if you are desperate for a beer after the climb.

Walk 21, page 51, para 2, line 10: For a short cut avoiding most of the bypass; about five minutes along the lane there is a staggered crossroad with signs to 'Center' and 'Anaxos'. Turn left here, walk up to the bypass and turn right. The track to Lafionas is about 40m on the left, just after a large new pale blue agricultural building.

Para 3: A new track has been opened up into an olive grove. Coming from Anaxos the track to Lafionas is now the third on the right.

Page 52, last para: There is a large new water-trough shortly before the junction.

Walk 22, page 53, para 3: The first sentence should read: 'Take the left-hand street out of the square into the village, and almost immediately the first turning on the left. Follow it as it bends round to the right.....'

The sign on the electricity pole has disappeared (there are various new signs around the village indicating the 'road' route to Ag. Alexandros) Several of the way marks have faded into near invisibility, but the path remains clear.

Page 54, para 2: The fountain has now been removed.

Para 3: Ignore the new track forking down to the right just after the monastery, unless you want an extra ten minute walk to a promontory with views over towards Skoutaros.

Walk 23, page 56, para 3: The foot of the first uphill track has washed out and is easily missed; the second is almost at the brow of the hill near the seat.

Para 5, line 1: There is new sign here to Λαφιώνα - Lafiona.
The sign at the next fork has been corrected with a taped arrow pointing right to Ag Alexandros.

Walk 26: page 61, para 3: Beyond the waymark the path has been widened into a rough track (an extension of the one at the foot of the page, which now winds down from side to side of the valley) After a few minutes it bends right across the stream and doubles back uphill. The original path continues ahead on the left-hand side of the stream.

Para 5: The new track crosses the path again at this point, between the two giant trees. Follow it up to the left and sharply round to the right. At the next left-hand bend the Turkish fountain is on the right. Then continue from the top of page 62.

Page 62, para 4: The gate and warning signs at the top of the track have been removed - there is now no obstacle to getting to the summit of Vigla. The communications post looks abandoned, though there are still radio sets in place and the door remains locked.

Page 63, last line: Add 'In five minutes turn left again at another T'

Page 64, paras 2-4: New brushwood barriers have made it necessary to reroute this section, as follows: 'The path leads back into trees and descends again. It bends round to the right and climbs on kalderimi. Go through a gate and bear left, with the entrance to an olive grove straight ahead. Climb steeply over a brow and down again with a wall on the right. In five minutes, continue ahead onto an overgrown path along a terrace wall. After two minutes bear right past a fallen tree and continue along the path with steep terracing down on the right towards the sea.

In another five minutes, by an entrance on the left over a fallen wall into an olive grove, go straight ahead along an overgrown kalderimi running between walls. Bear right and continue slightly uphill. Go along the path as it reverts to kalderimi leading down and across a stream, then bending right under a high stone wall on the other side. (This last section has become very overgrown) It finally bends left and climbs twenty metres to join a dirt road by a small trekking trail sign'

Page 66, last para: The previous top of the path and part of the fence has been washed away. Now leave the road immediately after the right-hand bend as the trekking trail sign comes into view.

The next printed update will be produced in early 2006. For a free copy send an addressed envelope to the address below.

If you come across anything that you think should be noted, please let me know by email or letter.

For interim updates and additional routes go to www.lesvoswalks.net

Published in January 2005 at:

The Olive Press

by M Maunder
R6 Marine Gate, Marine Drive
Brighton BN2 5TN, UK
email: mike@lesvoswalks.net
phone +44 (0)1273 675434

For more about Lesvos visit my website
www.lesvoswalks.net

On Foot in North Lesvos

Contents

Mithimna or Molivos?

The original name of the city-state which ruled this area of Lesvos was Mithimna or Methimna (Μήθυμνα). Founded in the 9th or 10th century BC, it was second only to Mitilene among the six states which divided the island. (The others were Eressos, Antissa - now reduced to a few remains on the coast north-east of the modern town - Pyrra, on the Gulf of Kalloni, and Arisbi, today a suburb of Kalloni on the main road to Mitilene).

During the Byzantine period it became known as Molivos (Μόλιβος), which it remained throughout the Turkish occupation from 1462 until 1912. Since then the official name of the town has reverted to Mithimna, which is the name used throughout this book. The persistence of the name Molivos is now largely due to the travel companies and their clients on whom the modern prosperity of the town is based.

Mithimna: The Donkey Station

All the walks starting from Mithimna (Μήθυμνα/Μόλιβος) begin at 'The Donkey Station'. To find this, take either of the roads leading away from the sea in the bus stop/school/taxi rank area at the beginning of the town. Where the two roads meet at the brow of the hill continue away from the sea for a few yards to the junction with the castle road running uphill to the left (sign posted Kastro). On your right at this point, opposite the Alonia Taverna, there is a pine wood (a public park) which used to be the starting point for donkey trekking excursions during the holiday season. Hence it is known to everyone in Mithimna as 'The Donkey Station'. (The donkey treks now start from the donkey farm - see Walk 3 for the location)

Petra

Walks from Petra (Πέτρα) start at the sea front square by the taxi rank.

Introduction

The Book

This book started life in the winter of 1999. I had first visited Mithimna in the spring of 1996, fallen in love with the town and surrounding countryside, and returned regularly in the years following. As I explored more, I became increasingly aware of the lack of up-to-date information for walkers: what little had been available seemed to be either out of print or out of date.

So I decided to spend the first winter of my retirement writing down my own favourites. By the spring of 2000 I had fourteen routes. I organised them into book form, printed a hundred copies on my home computer, and brought them to Mithimna with no real expectation of selling more than a few dozen. However by the end of my first morning I had sold out: I spent the rest of my stay avoiding shopkeepers demanding more, and the rest of the summer trying to catch up with orders.

For 2001 I added three more routes and Dutch and German translations; for this edition there are a further ten new routes, while two of the originals have been dropped, leaving twenty-six walks of varying lengths to choose from.

This remains a one-man operation: I find and annotate the routes, convert my notes into, I hope, clear descriptions, and check them at least once a year for changes on the ground. All these routes are described as they were in 2002. I can accept no responsibility for any difficulties you may encounter as a result of subsequent changes, or for any other reason. However, if you find anything that you think should be noted, or have any other suggestions, please write or email me at the addresses on the copyright page.

The Walks

The walks described are routes I have discovered while exploring the local countryside. With a few exceptions, they are walks, not 'treks', mainly along well-defined tracks or footpaths, and calling for no special clothing or equipment (I normally walk in shorts and trainers; on the rare occasions where heavier clothing is called for I mention it in the text). They are also all well within the capabilities of an unathletic but reasonably fit sixty-three year old like myself.

Most of the routes are point-to-point rather than circular, and can, of course, be walked in either direction. In most cases two or more walks can be combined into a circuit: I give a few suggestions at the end of the book, but there are many more permutations.

It is advisable to try one or two of the shorter walks first, to measure your speed and stamina against mine, before tackling the longer routes. Also please read through the descriptions of each walk before setting out and judge its length and difficulty against your and your party's capabilities. Most of my walking is done in May or October; in midsummer, July and August, it can get <u>very</u> hot and shade will be in short supply. Allow time for a slower pace and more rests, take plenty of water and be aware of the danger of overheating and dehydration. Also the vegetation will be tinder-dry; be especially careful not to start any fires.

Times and Distances

In the introduction to each walk I give the approximate overall time for its completion, with point-to-point times from one landmark to the next included in the description. Timings are to the nearest five minutes at a reasonably brisk walking pace, and do not include stops to rest, admire the view etc. For any times under five minutes where you might otherwise miss a turning I give a (very approximate) distance.

For the record my average walking speed over normal terrain is about three miles per hour. Because most walks zigzag up, down and around hillsides, however, translating times into even approximate distances is difficult if not impossible (and in any case fairly pointless), as is any attempt to measure the routes on any available map.

Which brings us on to:

Maps, Security and a little History

Until recently, for security reasons because of the island's proximity to Turkey, the only maps of Lesvos available to the public either in Greece or the UK were tourist maps which, to put it as tactfully as possible, are of variable accuracy and little use to walkers. In early 2000 restrictions were relaxed enough to allow ROAD Editions of Athens to publish an accurate and up-to-date 1:70000 scale map of the island. This is useful for reference, though the scale is too small for detailed use by walkers: few of the tracks and none of the paths used in these walks are shown.

For this reason I have tried to make the descriptions in this book detailed enough to make maps and other aids such as compasses superfluous. The map in the centre pages, based with thanks on the ROAD Editions map, is there simply as an approximate indication of directions and distances for use when planning your walks.

Security considerations also mean that the north coast of Lesvos facing the Asia Minor shore of Turkey little more than five miles away is heavily defended: unexplained mounds or holes in the ground that you may encounter on your walks will in all probability be military installations that should on no account be photographed; for the same reason they will not be mentioned in the descriptions that follow.

All this may seem like paranoia towards a country that is supposed to be Greece's NATO ally. However it is worth remembering that it was not until 1912 that Lesvos was liberated from 450 years of Turkish occupation, and that as one of the richest and strategically most important territories it was ruled at times more oppressively than many of the smaller and more remote islands.

Furthermore the disastrous failed attempt, encouraged by the British government of the time, to take advantage of Turkish weakness after the First World War to reclaim the ethnically Greek settlements of Asia Minor resulted in a resumption of war with atrocities on both sides culminating in the 'population exchange' of 1922-23. Sanctioned by the Treaty of Lausanne, this would today be described, more harshly and accurately, as ethnic cleansing. Nearly 400000 Turks and other Muslims still living in Greece were expelled, in exchange for up to 1.3 million people of Greek descent from Asia Minor. Of these about 15000 settled permanently in Lesvos; thus the parents and grandparents of a substantial proportion of today's (declining) population of 83000 were born across the straits in Asia Minor, victims of Greece's "Asia Minor Catastrophe"   The novels by the Lesvos author Stratis Myrivilis, 'The Mermaid Madonna' and 'The Schoolmistress with the Golden Eyes', set in Skala Sikaminia and Mithimna respectively, are set in the aftermath of the catastrophe, as is Dido Sotiriou's 'Farewell Anatolia' All are available in Mithimna in English translations.

Some Definitions

Most of these walks are along **tracks**, unsurfaced, often steep and rough, but wide enough for a four-wheeled vehicle. These shade into **dirt-roads**, which are rapidly disappearing under tarmac, but where they survive carry cars, pick-ups, trucks and any other traffic except buses (mopeds and motorbikes go up and down anything)

Paths are well-defined footpaths, often walled and running between fields, unlike **goat-tracks**, which wander across fields and up and down hillsides. Some tracks and paths are still surfaced with cobbles, these are the ancient **kalderimia** which were the original drove-roads and thoroughfares between settlements before the coming of the motor vehicle and the bulldozer. Note however that paths running across fields or mountainsides are on private land and are there for the benefit of the farmer - they are not rights of way. I have not asked permission to include these paths in this book and landowners have the right to restrict or prevent access for any reason. For your own sake and that of other walkers, please do not do anything which might harm stock or land where you are walking, or anything else that might antagonise farmers or landowners.

Almost all land in this part of Lesvos is fenced or walled. Most **gates** are to keep stock in or mark property boundaries rather than keep people out, and may be used unless padlocked or firmly wired shut. They can be anything from a strand of barbed wire to a wrought-iron creation set between stone pillars; most popular are lengths of concrete reinforcing mesh and old single bed frames (which are just the right size for a gate across a track). As you would anywhere, always leave them as you find them.

Similarly, **farm buildings** can range from large modern concrete cattle-sheds through ancient stone byres to sheds pieced together from scrap timber and sheet metal.

River- and stream-beds are usually dry, or carrying only a trickle of water, during the holiday season from May to October. In the wet season, from late October on, or after unseasonable storms, however, they can become torrents or subject to flash floods. If you are planning a walk that involves crossing, or walking along, a stream-bed, take extra care in unfavourable weather.

Flora and Fauna

This is not intended to be a wildlife guide, and I have not attempted to identify the plants and animals that you may meet, beyond the obvious trees; oaks, pines, and the ubiquitous olives used as landmarks. Efstathiadis of Athens publishes well-illustrated field guides to wild flowers, trees, birds, etc. in several languages, which are available in local bookshops.

Greek vegetation, almost by definition, is aggressive. It has spikes, spines and thorns and will use them on any unprotected flesh, especially at ankle level. Particularly in summer, anything described as 'pasture' or 'meadow' will consist almost entirely of thorn bushes and thistles. And if those don't get you the holly oak will!

Most wild animals will sense you before you see them, and get out of your way. You may see red squirrels, and if you are very lucky a pine marten. There are tortoises, terrapins and frogs in ponds and cisterns, and of course lizards of various sizes and colours everywhere. There is one poisonous snake in Lesvos, a variety of adder, but you are unlikely to come a live one except possibly as a rustling in the undergrowth as you pass.

Lesvos is a paradise for bird-watchers, as it is on spring and autumn migration routes, but if you are a bird-watcher you will know this already.

Dogs, of course, are everywhere. Like their owners, the vast majority of island dogs are friendly: the frantic barking of a tethered dog more often comes from boredom and a wish for attention than from aggressiveness. (And in my experience if you say a kind word to an untethered dog you are likely to have it as a companion for the next mile or more of your walk). However it is of course sensible to use normal caution when dealing with them.

Guard Dogs of Mithimna

Local Transport

During the holiday season a shuttle bus service runs along the coast between Eftalou and Anaxos. The main service bus from Mithimna to Mitilene via Petra and Kalloni runs anything from one to six times a day depending on the season, day of the week, school and public holidays etc. The tourist information office next door to the National Bank of Greece in Mithimna usually has the current timetable posted in the window, and can advise on changes. (The main KTEΛ bus summer timetable for Lesvos is also posted on the internet (at http://www.lesvosonline.gr/Lesvos/ Map/transp/buses.htm), but this can be subject to change). Buses to villages off the main road, even quite large places such as Stipsi, tend to be infrequent, and organised as feeder services connecting at Kalloni.

Taxis, however, as everywhere in Greece, are plentiful, convenient, and relatively cheap. There are taxi stands at

Mithimna (phone 22530 71480) and Petra (22530 42022 or 22530 41169). Stipsi, Pelopi, and Ypsilometopo all have their own taxis.

Other Walks

The Lesviots, like most people who have relied on the land for their living, have been slow to understand the idea of country walking for pleasure. However there are now a number of initiatives planned or under way, of which the most visible at the time of writing is the EU Leader project sponsored 'Olive Paths of Lesvos'. Information boards and route maps are appearing at strategic points across the north-east of the island, featuring walking routes mainly on dirt roads. And throughout the island there are networks of unsurfaced forest and mountain roads, shown in detail on the ROAD Editions map (Sheet 212, Lesbos) offering almost. completely uninterrupted peace and spectacular views.

And Finally

Above all, don't be afraid to explore. All the walks here are the result of my thinking 'I wonder where that goes', and going to find out. Many, indeed most, tracks and paths will turn out to be dead ends, but you will come across more views, more wildlife, and maybe some interesting people. And it is very difficult to get completely lost; there will almost always be a visible landmark, or the sea, to aim for. So:

Safe and Happy Walking!

'He who drinks the water, forgets it not and returns'

Walk 1
Mithimna Ancient and Modern

Walking time about 1½ hours, but allow a full morning to visit the castle, browse, stop and stare, sit in tavernas etc.

The Mithimna area has been continuously settled since the Bronze Age, first in the valley running down to the sea to the east of the town, now occupied by the Aphrodite Hotel. From about the middle of the thirteenth century BC the city grew on its present site, plus the plateau of the Dapia, behind the harbour, in all about double the area of the modern town:-

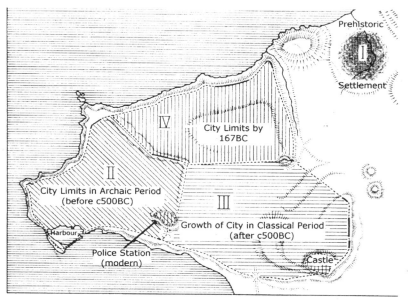

Looked at from below the main street of Mithimna (ΟΔΟΣ 17 ΝΟΕΜΒΡΙΟΥ - 17 November or ΑΓΟΡΑ - Market) runs across the cliff like a giant bow, with the harbour road as the bowstring. From the highest point of the bow ΟΔΟΣ ΚΑΣΤΡΟΥ (Castle Street), continues diagonally upwards towards the castle. Above and to the right of these streets a maze of cobbled lanes, terraces and staircases rises steeply up to the castle, filled with houses large and small, old and new. Strict controls ensure that new buildings in the town conform to traditional styles, and rapidly blend in with their surroundings: for instance the OTE telephone exchange on

*the harbour road and the health centre in ΟΔΟΣ ΚΑΣΤΡΙΟΥ were
both built as recently as 1999. The best way to discover this part
of town is to spend a morning getting lost in it, remembering that
heading downhill will always (eventually) bring you back to the
main street or the school.*

*This walk explores the other quarters of old and new Mithimna,
with plenty of opportunities for relaxing with a drink, or being
tempted by the wide variety of specialist shops along the way.
Time it so that you arrive at the castle during opening hours -
normally 0800 - 1900 daily (except Mondays) during the summer
season.*

From the donkey station, take the road opposite leading uphill,
signposted to the castle (Κάστρο). At the first bend to the right cut
off the hairpin by taking the steps straight ahead past the entrance
to the small cemetery. Continue on the road as it zigzags uphill,
with views to the right towards the sea and Eftalou, the
Lepetymnos mountain range, and nearer, the solitary remaining
tower of the Roman aqueduct that once supplied Mithimna with
water. Still rising, the road swings round under a pine wood on the
hill to the left (on top of which are the water cisterns which supply
the town today) and arrives at the castle.

The castle as it survives
today is mainly
Byzantine, built on the
site of much more
ancient fortifications
dating from the 9th or
10th century BC. It was
repaired and extended in
1373AD by Francisco
Gattelusi, the Genoese
ruler of Lesvos of the
time, and later by the
Turkish occupiers of the
island. Note the Turkish
inscription that survives over the entrance gate. The panoramic
views from the castle walls towards the interior of the island and
across the strait to the Turkish coast, (though not recommended to

any sufferer from vertigo), are in themselves worth the admission charge.

On leaving the castle return along the path past the Panorama taverna and follow the street running downhill on its right. Take the second turning to the left opposite the street sign ΟΔΟΣ ΚΑΣΤΡΟΥ and continue down the stepped street to a crossing with a bakery on the left. The main shopping street lies ahead under a canopy of vines awaiting our return but for now we turn right into ΟΔΟΣ ΑΡΓΥΡΗ ΕΦΤΑΛΙΩΤΗ (Argilis Eftaliotis, the modern Greek poet, whose bust is in the forecourt of the municipal art gallery, and whose house, with a plaque beside the gate, is a few yards down this street on the left.

Continue down through ΠΛΑΤΕΙΑ ΑΝΔΡΕΑ ΚΥΡΙΑΚΟΥ (Andrea Kyriakos Square) where two massive trees give shade to the open air Tropicana Taverna and the two impressive nineteenth century mansions in their walled gardens to the right, and take the next right turn into ΟΔΟΣ ΔΙΟΚΗΤΗΡΙΟΥ (Diokitirios), signposted to the Police Station (ΑΣΤΥΝΟΜΙΑ). Pass ancient remains on the left opposite another mansion on the right, and then the police station on the left, built on a rock outcrop and remains of the ancient city wall. Wrought iron gates lead on to a paved road which curves away right towards a cemetery. At the second electricity pole on the left follow a track across the field to pass the remains of an ancient round windmill on the right and then into the next field.

This area is all part of the Dapia, the site of the ancient city of Mithimna, stretching from the castle to Cape Molivos, which lies ahead. In 1895 a British archaeologist, W H D Rouse, noted that "Between the fortress and the sea is a wide stretch of land, the site of the old town, covered with thousands of potsherds and pieces of earthen ware", and this remains true today.   Over the centuries the area has been continuously cultivated and the remains scattered, but some sites are identifiable and have been partially excavated. One lies about twenty yards ahead, where the remains of an old courtyard, walls, pavement and well can be seen.

From the well, follow the line of the courtyard towards a small headland. The cliff to the left of this appears to be the site of an old rubbish dump, with large quantities of broken pottery visible in the eroding cliff face and on the beach below. Near the top of the cliff lie two large blocks of worked masonry, identified by archaeologists as being from the ancient city walls.

Now follow the cliff-top path to the right as it leads through a gap in a fence and round to Cape Molivos. Beyond the cape the path continues to another partial excavation of ancient buildings on the right.

Walk away from the sea along the line of the main excavated wall. A faint path leads up to the cemetery wall ahead. Take this and then follow the wall right until it joins the raised road, where there is a protruding stone step. *(This field becomes very overgrown with thistles during the summer. Those wearing shorts may find it easier to retrace their steps back to the road.)*

Return up the road. At the point where the walk originally left the road take a footpath to the right (at about 45° above the track) past a wall on the left topped with pine trees leading to a small gate and steps down to the street. Turn right (there is an excavation in progress of an impressive Roman villa or baths in the small paddock to the left at this point) and follow down to the harbour, turning right on to the street (not the narrow alleyway) at the bottom of the hill.

Take a while to explore the harbour (there is a water fountain in the wall beyond The Captain's Table (ΤΟ ΤΡΑΠΕΖΙ ΤΟΥ ΚΑΠΕΤΑΝΙΟΥ) taverna, one of the few remaining with its original Turkish inscription, and a small boatyard at the end of the quay where the local fishing caïques are repaired and built) and its galleries and tavernas. Then follow round the outer harbour - the quay here is where the larger fishing boats unload their catch every

evening - past the harbour church, Ag. Nikolaos, and back up the harbour road as it climbs along the cliff, with views to Vafios and along the beach to the Olive Press and beyond.

In the rear wall of the courtyard to the left of the OTE telephone exchange is a section of Lesvian polygonal masonry from the Archaic period, with more lining the underground chamber in front. If the courtyard is closed this is visible from the lane behind, accessible from the steps to the right of 'Dilino' restaurant, next to another fountain, this time with inscriptions in both Turkish and Greek, commemorating the donor as ΧΑΤΣΙΑΧΜΕΤΟΓΛΟΥ ΧΑΤΣΙΜΟΥΣΤΑΦΑ (Hatsiachmetoglu Hatsimustapha) in 1884.

Where the paved harbour road becomes tarmac and begins to run downhill take the cobbled fork left uphill leaving the Sansibal restaurant on the right. Keep right as the road climbs diagonally up the cliff, past the municipal art gallery (ΔΗΜΟΤΙΚΗ ΠΙΝΑΚΟΘΗΚΗ) and the bust of ΑΡΓΥΡΗ ΕΦΤΑΛΙΩΤΗ (Argilis Eftaliotis) on the left. Continue up under a canopy of vines through shops, cafenions and tavernas to the junction with ΟΔΟΣ ΚΑΣΤΡΙΟΥ. This is the centre of the town; to the right is the community hall, built on the site of the Turkish mosque and bridging over the street, with a well and water troughs in the forecourt and the remains of the minaret on the wall above.

Further up ΟΔΟΣ ΚΑΣΤΡΙΟΥ on the right, almost hidden behind gift shops, are the Turkish public baths. A marble-tiled foyer leads into an antechamber under a pierced domed roof, and thence into an impressive circular bathhouse, the walls lined with individual cubicles in white marble and with a marble floor, all under a large pierced dome.

(NB Unfortunately, these baths are currently closed for safety reasons due to structural dilapidation. There are plans, and funds,

for their restoration, but for the moment it is only possible to snatch glimpses of the outside of the building from the open-air cafenion opposite the Post Office)

Finally, continue on up the hill to a gate on the left about ten yards beyond the Post Office. Go through on to the terrace of the church of Αγιος Παντελεήμων (St Panteleimon) to rest for a few minutes while you admire the views over the harbour and the bay of Mithimna.

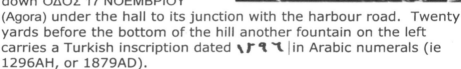

To return to the start of the walk at the donkey station walk back down ΟΔΟΣ 17 ΝΟΕΜΒΡΙΟΥ (Agora) under the hall to its junction with the harbour road. Twenty yards before the bottom of the hill another fountain on the left carries a Turkish inscription dated ١٢٩٦ |in Arabic numerals (ie 1296AH, or 1879AD).

Turn left and left again, with the school on your right and the excavated site of an ancient cemetery on your left, (there is more polygonal masonry visible here, dating these tombs too to the Archaic period) and continue up the hill to the donkey station.

Opposite the cemetery, the car park behind the school lies on the site of Mithimna's ancient theatre.

Walk 2
A Short Stroll through the Mithimna Olive Groves
Walking time 40 minutes

After a day on the beach this short, level, forty-minute stroll is just the thing to prepare for that pre-dinner drink or three.

From the donkey station take the track running down to the right of the pine wood and bear left on to a short stretch of concrete road. Pass the Liokambi apartment complex on the left.

Immediately after this the track divides by a small cottage on the left, with a walled track leading off to the right. Ignore this and continue on the walled path ahead, passing a stone barn on the right. The track zigzags left and right past gates into olive groves and a new house behind high wrought iron gates on the right.

Shortly after passing a white stone archway under a tiled roof on the left (which leads into another olive grove) turn right at a T onto the crossing track. *(For a shorter version of this walk turn left here)*

After about 20 yards the track passes a house on the right and continues to the river. (This is the river which passes under the Mithimna-Petra road at the twin bridges near the Vafios road junction and emerges into the sea halfway along Mithimna beach).

Follow the track as it swings left along the river bank with a cottage and garden wall on the left and turn left again at the next junction.

Continue with vegetable gardens on the right, go left where the track next divides, over a slight rise and then right at the T junction with a rock face on the left. *(The short cut rejoins here from the left)*

After another five minutes the pine wood will appear on the left and the sports ground on the right: the track emerges on to the road between the donkey station and the olive press belonging to the growers' co-operative.

Walk 3
A Circuit through the Hills behind Mithimna
Walking time about 1¼ hours

The paths and tracks criss-crossing through the hills behind Mithimna give a number of opportunities for shortish circular walks. Here are three suggestions.

From the donkey station take the track to the left of the pine wood. Where the track divides at a rock face (8 mins) turn left over the rise. After another two minutes there is a junction: carry straight on and follow the track as it bears round to the left.

At the next junction take the track to the right (5 mins). (Continuing straight ahead at this point will bring you back in 10 minutes to the Mithimna-Eftalou road, on the way passing the donkey farm belonging  to Michaelis, the leader of the donkey trekking excursions that start here)

After passing the gallops belonging to the Pegasus Equestrian Club of Mithimna   ΙΠΠΙΚΟΣ ΟΜΙΛΟΣ
ΜΗΘΥΜΝΑΣ
Ο ΠΗΓΑΣΟΣ   (10 mins) continue along the track with the river gorge on the right for another five minutes to farm buildings on the right, and then wind uphill, ignoring tempting tracks on the right and left, over a small ridge, and, ignoring another track joining from the left (this merely leads back to the farm buildings on top of the mound to the left, and stops), come to a T-junction with the track from Mithimna to the Argenos-Vafios road (20 mins).

Turn left here to return to Mithimna, following the main track as it hairpins down leaving the boundary of the Mithimna-Sikaminia nature reserve to the right. (Note the frequent signs forbidding hunting - ΑΠΑΓΟΡΕΥΕΤΑΙ ΤΟ ΚΥΝΗΓΙ) In particular ignore the first track to the left; this leads to the Mithimna municipal tip, and helps to explain the rubbish scattered along this section of the walk, and also the sign at the entrance to the farm enclosure at the next corner, ΑΠΑΓΟΡΕΥΕΤΑΙ Η ΡΙΨΗ ΜΠΑΖΩΝ - 'No Tipping'.

After 25 minutes the track passes the Camping Mithimna campsite on the left and joins the Mithimna-Eftalou road. Turn left, and if you wish follow the road back to the donkey station (10 mins).

Otherwise, after about fifty yards, where the road swings left, take the road leading off to the right with the castle ahead in the distance. Follow this road, which after a while loses its tarmac surface, ignoring turnings to right and left, as it skirts the foot of the mound crowned by the remains of the Roman aqueduct. Just

before another track joins from the other side of the mound a path leads off to the left. Take this and follow it as it runs between fields and passes a large animal shed on the right, before bending right and ending at a sloping rock-face. Bear right up across the rock for about fifty metres and then left to rejoin the path which leads between a fenced field on the left and a steep bank on the right up to the Mithimna Castle road at the bend by the cemetery (10 mins). To return to the donkey station turn left and walk down the road for five minutes.

Walk 4
A Longer Circuit
Walking time (a) 1 hour 50 minutes or (b) 1 hour 35 minutes

This is a longer and more adventurous version of Walk 3 which involves a short stretch of off-path scrambling down a hillside and stream bank.

Follow Walk 7 for fifteen minutes until you reach the brow of a small hill. Just beyond this turn left on to a track leading across the valley, through a gate and across a stream bed to a group of farm buildings on the opposite hillside (15 mins).

Continue through the farm, leaving the buildings on the left, and follow the path that winds up the hillside behind with Mithimna castle visible on the horizon to the left. Look for the remains of a round stone animal pen and leave this on your right. The path continues round the right-hand side of the hill and then down to an animal pen, where it ends (15 mins).

Go on towards the rock outcrop ahead, leaving it to the left and above. Work diagonally downhill, with a fence on the left, to the river below. Cross, and then follow a goat-track left towards the farm buildings visible on top of the bank ahead. Climb the bank into the farmyard and then go right on to the track to rejoin Walk 3 (20 mins). Turn right (a) to continue Walk 3, or left (b) to return to Mithimna (Walk 3 in reverse).

Walk 5
Hills, Valleys, and Sea
Walking time 2½ hours

This route is one of contrasts. After climbing along the rugged scrub covered valley behind Mithimna, you cross a ridge and descend towards Eftalou across pasture and through the shade of olive groves. Reaching the sea, there is a short stroll along the beach before the final section past market gardens and smallholdings.
NB In late summer/early autumn nets are laid in the olive groves in preparation for the winter harvest. The ground is completely covered, and therefore this walk is only possible earlier in the year.

From the donkey station take the track to the left of the pine wood and follow Walk 3 for the first 45 minutes.

At the T-junction turn left towards the smallholdings and metal farm buildings that line the left-hand side of the track, but after about 30 metres go through a gate on the right leading towards an older stone farm building, and then immediately right again on to a rough track leading downhill.

This track soon
ends; take the
right-hand path
(there is another
leading ahead
round the side of
the hill to the left)
which runs
downhill bending

left to a stony ridge with a small rocky outcrop on the left (5 mins). Carry on down the stony path towards the valley for another five minutes, passing a water-trough on the left and ruined stone sheepfold on the right.

Bear left and follow the path down round the end of a wall and through scattered olive and fig trees. It continues left (at about 10 o'clock - along this stretch several sheep-tracks divide and converge but all lead in the same general direction) through pasture, across a small stream, and through a gap in a low tumble-down wall (7 mins).

The path is now well-defined once more, leading through a group of oak trees and in five minutes reaching a track.

Cross the track diagonally to the left and continue on the path opposite, which after two minutes leads through a wall under an oak tree. It divides by more oaks but soon comes together again; the higher, left-hand option is easier and clearer to follow. Follow it left under a larger oak and then down right into an olive grove. Bear left down the terracing, with the stone terrace wall on the right at 1 o'clock (5 mins). Go right and down again, then sharp left round the end of a terrace wall and down another level. Now go right and follow the path downhill to the right through a wall and shrubs - oak on the left, holly-oak on the right (5 mins).

Immediately bear left and continue down. Go down a steep bank under an old olive tree on to a clear path bearing left through yet more terracing to a level olive-grove below. Continue straight ahead for another five minutes to come out on the bank of a river (or more likely riverbed) running between stone walls.

Follow the path left along the left bank of the river for about five minutes, passing a rock outcrop on the left and over a short rocky stretch, until the riverbed becomes a concrete road and the path drops down to join it.

Continue through a gate and on down the road for another five minutes to join the Eftalou beach road.

Turn left along the road for five minutes, past the fisherman's shack and one-boat mini harbour, and go down the concrete ramp to the beach opposite the Panselinos (ΠΑΝΣΕΛΗΝΟΣ) hotel/apartments.

Walk along the narrow beach for about ten minutes (warning - if there is a strong offshore wind you may get wet feet).

Turn left off the beach onto a track (there is a sign here to the Restaurant Tsipouri). A short distance up the track there is an old

Turkish water fountain on the left, followed by the entrance to the Hotel Elpis on the right. When the track forks after this, go right past the entrance to the Restaurant Tsipouri (On old maps this area is called Tsipouri. Tsipouro is a drink similar to raki, distilled in the home from vine stems, figs, or mulberries, so possibly there were orchards here) Continue uphill through fields, and pass the overgrown rear entrance of the Pension Taverna Orpheus (ΟΡΦΕΑΣ) on the left.

The track continues to the right of the aqueduct tower. At the next junction (20 mins) turn left and immediately right on to a path. This runs between fields and passes a large animal shed on the right, before bending right and ending at a sloping rock-face. Bear right up across the rock for about fifty metres and then left to rejoin the path which leads between a fenced field on the left and a steep bank on the right up to the Mithimna Castle road at the bend by the cemetery (10 mins). To return to the donkey station turn left and walk down the road for five minutes.

Walk 6
Through the Hills from Mithimna to Petra
Walking time 1½ hours

*Everyone on holiday in Mithimna visits Petra at least once, to visit
the church on the rock from which the village takes its name, the
Panagia Glykophiloussa (Παναγίας της Γλυκοφιλούσας) - Our Lady of
the Sweet Kiss, the c18 Macedonian-style Valeltzidaina mansion,
and, of course, the long sandy beach. This walk, and the next,
give two alternative routes avoiding the main coast road, and can
be combined to make a circular expedition.*

Take the track to
the right of the
donkey station, as
in Walk 2, but
where the path
divides at the
cottage beyond the
Liokambi
apartments turn
right onto the
walled track, which

leads between the olive groves and orchards until after about ten
minutes it arrives at the river bank. Cross the river bed and follow
the track on the opposite bank until it joins the Mithimna-Vafios
road (5 mins).

Cross the road and go through the gate opposite *(this land has
been for sale as a building plot - ΠΩΛΟΥΝΤΑΙ ΟΙΚΟΠΕΔΑ - so it is
possible that this access may change),* and follow the path, leaving
to the left the holiday apartments of the Pension Marianthi and
then a small chapel on a mound. Continue along the well-defined
path through fields and scrubland, through a gate and on with a
line of oak trees on the left (5 mins).

The path bears left with farm buildings visible to the right, and
continues through rougher ground and denser scrub to another
gate. The rear entrance to an enclosed estate is visible just ahead
(5 mins). *(This is Karuna, a private holiday centre used for
spiritual retreats. The owners and guests value their privacy and
isolation - **please respect it by keeping out of the property)***

Beyond the gate the path leads ahead outside the boundary of the estate as far as its main entrance. Take the track leading away from the gates and then immediately turn right through a gate on to a track running uphill (10 mins). *(The main track leads down to the Mithimna-Petra track near the reservoir - see Walk 7)*

Continue up the hill. Ignore the track to the right, which leads to farm buildings, from which it is possible to cross a field to another track running back to join the coast road at the Aegean Sea Studios.

The uphill track bends left and continues to climb under woodland. Pass through a gate and after a few yards turn right. Continue along this track, climbing gently through trees along the seaward side of the ridge. (There are several tempting tracks leading off uphill to the left along this stretch. They are all dead ends leading to the top of the ridge and no further, but provide stunning views over the bay of Petra and the hills behind).

Eventually, after ten minutes, follow the track as it forks right and goes steeply downhill. (This stretch is very steep and rough and should be treated with care, though a concrete surface was laid on parts of it during 2002 to allow trucks to reach a hilltop construction site). It zigzags down and goes through a gate to join the main Mithimna-Petra coast road at an acute angle above Petra harbour (25 mins).

Turn left on to the road and follow it down until it swings right at the bottom of the hill. Join the beach and walk along to Petra's main square with its tavernas and shops (20 mins).

The taxi rank is also here for anyone wanting a ride home. The bus stop is about 200 metres along the road towards Mithimna, outside the public car-park.

(If you intend to continue on Walks 14 or 15 and do not wish to stop in the centre of Petra, turn off the beach opposite the OTE building and follow the track to its right. When this joins the Petra-Kalloni road turn right on to the road for five minutes until you reach the road to Petri on the left at 'The Grand Café')

Walk 7
Mithimna to Petra via the Reservoir
Walking time 1¼ hours

This is a shorter and easier route than Walk 6, and is what holiday company representatives often suggest if asked about possible walks; that is if they don't recommend this book!

From the donkey station take the track to the left of the pine wood. Where the track divides at a rock face (8 mins) turn left over the rise and take the next track to the right.

Pass through vegetable gardens on the left and orchards and olive groves on the right, and at the next junction bear left. Cross a small river by a concrete bridge, and a little further on go over a small stream where it runs through a culvert. The track rises up through scrubby pasture to the brow of a small hill. Just beyond this a track leads off to the left across a valley; Walk 4 diverges here.

Continue along the main track to meet the Mithimna-Vafios road to the left of a block of studios (10 mins)

Turn left onto the road for about 200 yards and then take a wide track off to the right. (Look for a small sign to Petra 3km and a yellow mailbox for Karuna at the junction). After about five minutes the track to Karuna turns off to the right; there is a yellow sign to Karuna and another blue sign pointing ahead to Petra 2.5km. Shortly after this pass to the left of the reservoir and begin to climb gently with woodland on the right.

Look out for blue arrows on rocks on the left indicating a path to Vafios, and also pointing back to Molivos. This is where Walk 10 joins the track. (15 mins)

Follow the track as it starts to descend and drops down to the right between two ponds, ignoring both the track leading off to the left through a gate (which leads into a small quarry), and the one leading straight ahead. The ponds may be dry later in the summer but in spring are home to frogs and terrapins which can sometimes be surprised basking on the banks. Continue down and follow the track round to the right, again ignoring the gated track on the left.

Pass the entrance to ΠΕΤΡΑ ΦΑΡΜ on the right and continue straight ahead, ignoring all side tracks, to meet the Petra-Kalloni road.

NB: Coming from Petra, take the left-hand road at this point. The road off to the right (at about one o'clock) leads across the plain, past Petra's new high school (ΓΥΜΝΑΣΙΟ) and college (ΛΥΚΕΙΟ) and then up to the St Constantine (Αγ Κωνσταντίνος) crossing (see page 35).

If you are intending to continue to Petri or beyond on Walks 14-16 and do not wish to visit Petra, turn left here and walk up the main road for five minutes to turn left again at 'The Grand Café' and join them there.

Cross the road and follow the track opposite (the local buses sometimes use the entrance as a parking space) until it emerges on the Petra beach road between the OTE building on the right and Stratos restaurant on the left.

Turn left and walk along past the bus stop to the village square (25 mins).

Walk 8
Through the Valleys from Mithimna to Vafios
Walking time 2 hours

This walk leads up through the valleys running south-east from Mithimna up towards the Lepetymnos mountains, alongside the Mithimna-Sikaminea nature reserve. This route is the one followed by the donkey-trekking expeditions to Vafios, so do not be surprised to be passed by (or overtake) a string of donkeys ridden by anxious holidaymakers under the supervision of Michaelis on his horse.

From the donkey station take the road uphill towards the castle. It bends right (there are steps ahead) to lead round a small cemetery and then left again. Leave the road at the apex of the left-hand bend and go down a footpath with a bank on the left and a field on the right. The path soon opens out on to a sloping rock face; go diagonally down to the right and pick the path up again at the bottom right-hand corner. Follow it along, keeping left where it forks by a small wellhead, and continue past a large animal shed on the left. Fifteen minutes from the start the path ends near the junction of three tracks below a mound crowned with the remains of a masonry pillar, (the one surviving part of the 4th century BC Roman aqueduct which once brought water to Mithimna from the springs of Lepetymnos).

Go right and follow the track (which becomes a tarmac road) ignoring side-tracks to tavernas etc. to join the Mithimna-Eftalou road, and follow it for about fifty yards until it swings left. (10 mins)

(If you wish, you can skip this first section by following the Eftalou road from the donkey station to this junction.)

Carry straight on up a side road, past a sign on the left marking the boundary of the nature reserve, and the 'Camping Mithymna'

site on the right. Continue past the 'No Entry' sign as the road becomes a track. Note the ΑΠΑΓΟΡΕΥΕΤΑΙ ΤΟ ΚΥΝΗΓΙ (Hunting Forbidden) signs on the left, which will be repeated at intervals along the length of the track as it skirts the boundary of the nature reserve.

The track runs up the side of the valley with views of the sea and across to the Turkish coastline on the left. It divides, with the left fork leading down into the valley (10 mins).

Follow the main, right-hand path up round right- and left-hand hairpins leaving a white concrete building on the left and the entrance to a farm enclosure on the right (there is a sign here ΑΠΑΓΟΡΕΥΕΤΑΙ Η ΡΙΨΗ ΜΠΑΖΩΝ - No Tipping). It continues to climb round another right-hand hairpin past a track to the right leading to the municipal rubbish tip. Don't take this track!!; continue on the main one left past animal pens and farm buildings. It starts to climb again and an alternative route from Mithimna (Walk 3) enters from the right (15 mins).

The track now runs approximately west-east along the right-hand side of the valley as it rises towards a ridge, which it crosses (15 mins) and continues up the left-hand side of the next valley, with wooded slopes ahead and opposite falling into the stream below.

If you follow the track for another half-hour it will lead you to the Vafios - Argenos road, where a right turn and another half-hour will bring you to Vafios.

Instead of this, where the track bends back to the left after crossing the ridge, go straight ahead to the left of rocks and a metal sheepfold and follow a path leading diagonally to the right down into the foot of the valley (5 mins).

Cross the stream and go through the small gate on the far side. Follow the path up through thorn bushes, and where it meets another at a T-junction go right. In five minutes, at a ridge, bear left. The path runs along the left-hand side of a valley, over a small bluff and then down through a small open area and more thorn bushes to another stream.

Cross, go through the gate on the far side and follow the path uphill to an opening into a meadow on the right (10 mins). (This short stretch is rocky and muddy in places - it doubles as a stream-bed)

Follow the path up the left-hand edge of the meadow to the top, then go between rocks into a second field and carry on to a brushwood gate at its top left-hand corner. Go through and through a second gate diagonally left across a narrow track. (5 mins).

On the right there is a low stone building housing a 'walk-in' water cistern, and diagonally right across the field is the chapel of St John (Αγ Ιωάννις). Walk up through the field to the track at the top and follow it left up to the road (10 mins).

Turn right on to the road by a large single storey white building.

(Opposite there is a track leading diagonally off to the left. This zigzags about halfway up the mountainside, from where a combination of goat-tracks, stream-beds and scrambling will eventually bring you to the television and radio masts above on the top of Profitis Ilias. Despite its name, traditionally in  *Greece given to the highest point in an island or region, this is not, quite, the highest peak in the range, at 957m (3140ft) being marginally lower than the 968m (3176ft) of Vigla*

two kilometres to the north-east. From Profitis Ilias a track leads down the southern face of the range to Pelopi, the ancestral village of Michael Dukakis, the 1988 US Presidential candidate.)

Follow the road for another ten minutes to the outskirts of Vafios and then take a concrete road (signpost Βαφειός) as it leads off uphill to the left. It becomes stone paved and leads to a T-junction. Turn right and immediately left to the cafenions in the village square. (5 mins)

To continue to Stipsi on Walk 11 continue ahead through the square, otherwise turn right downhill through the village to rejoin the main road as it bends downhill by a small playground, and walk down to the neighbouring tavernas, Taverna Vafios and Taverna Ilias. (5 mins)

Walk 9
Mithimna to Vafios through Keramotis
Walking time 2¼ hours

*Although the village of Vafios is only three miles from Mithimna it is comparatively untouched by tourism, apart from the two tavernas on the road which runs below it. This is a fairly strenuous walk, **part of which runs along a valley used as rifle ranges, and for occasional artillery exercises. Obviously while shooting is in progress it is not possible to walk this part of the route; in any case proceed with caution, and if in any doubt, don't!** A sign at the entrance from the Mithimna - Vafios road reads*

ΚΙΝΔΥΝΟΣ
ΑΠΟ ΜΗ ΕΚΡΑΓΕΝΤΑ
ΒΛΗΜΑΤΑ
ΜΗΝ ΕΓΓΙΖΕΤΕ
ΤΥΧΟΝ ΒΛΗΜΑΤΑ
ΕΙΔΟΠΟΙΗΕΤΕ
ΣΤΡΑΤΙΩΤΙΚΗ Η ΑΣΤΥΝΟΜΙΚΗ
ΑΡΧΗ

*"Danger from unexploded shells. Do not touch any shells. Inform the Military Police Authority" **You have been warned!!** When firing is in progress it is clearly audible from the town, and should allow you to change your plans if necessary.*

Follow Walk 3 for the first thirty minutes as far as the farm buildings on the right, then continue on the track as it winds uphill.

In five minutes the track bends sharp left and a secondary track goes off at an acute angle to the right. Take this and follow it down to farm buildings in the valley (before it dries up in the summer there is a small waterfall in the oleander-lined stream below to the right of the track). Go round to the left of the buildings and through a small gate leading diagonally down to the stream. Cross the stream - there is a makeshift footbridge, or if you prefer, stepping stones immediately down stream. (10 mins)

On the far side of the stream climb up through the rocks and pick up the small path leading to the right up the hillside. (From this point until the edge of the Keramotis valley a black plastic water pipe runs parallel to the path)

The path climbs across a rock-face, then after five minutes levels and bends left across the head of a valley. Carry on up between two rock outcrops and bear left; Mithimna is visible to the right on the right of a large outcrop. Wind up through grass and thorn bushes for another five minutes to the head of a gorge. Go left across a rock-face and then diagonally right across a patch of scree and follow the path up to a gap on the ridge ahead.

Go over the ridge and across the head of the next valley to the next ridge, then follow right towards a stone animal shed on the edge of a small pasture (5 mins).

Turn sharp left away from the building on to the path running gently down along the side of the valley (down on the right are the Keramotis ranges). After five minutes it turns right above the head of the valley and ends at a water-trough by a small gate (the black water-pipe disappears uphill to the left at this point).

Go through the gate and continue on a very faint path for about fifty metres, then turn down right to a small level open space, and left on to a track. Follow this along the side of the Keramotis valley, past the artillery points 4 and 5 down to the rifle range in the bottom of the valley, and cross to the end of the track opposite (10 mins).

(If you prefer a quicker and easier route to this point, walk up the Mithimna - Vafios road for about five minutes beyond the beginning of the track leading to the reservoir and Petra, to a track leading off to the left. The warning sign, stencilled black on yellow, is (or was in 2002) here. Twenty minutes along this track brings you to the end of the rifle range and the point above)

The track turns right and ends by a concrete hut; follow it and continue up a goat path towards a fence on the hillside, ignoring the track which runs around the head of the valley. Follow the line of the fence left to join the footpath which is visible on the hillside behind butts 12 and 13.

Follow the path down into a river valley. Cross the river and climb the opposite bank (15 mins). The path continues to climb ahead towards two trees, then bears right leaving a rocky outcrop and tree on the left. Leave another rock and tree on the right, then immediately go between two small trees and head towards the farm buildings visible to the left. Before reaching them the path comes on to the Mithimna-Vafios road. (5 mins)

Cross the road and take the track opposite to the right of the buildings (There is a sign here ΠΡΟΣΟΧΗ ΖΩΑ - Caution, Animals) Follow this track for ten minutes, alongside new stone walls to the right, until it rejoins the road.

Continue up the road to the right for about 200 yards, and when it swings right take the rough track leading off ahead and left. Follow it left, leaving a small chapel on the right, past cottages on the left, and re-emerge on the road at Taverna Ilias (ΤΑΒΕΡΝΑ Ο ΗΛΙΑΣ). (5 mins)

Follow the road uphill until it swings left by a small childrens' playground, and then take the steep street to the right of the playground up into the centre of Vafios village (10 mins).

Walk 10
From Vafios to the Mithimna-Petra track
Walking time 40 minutes

There are several short way-marked routes in the Mithimna-Petra area, created several years ago by a walking club based in Petra. This one leads through the hills below Vafios towards Petra to meet the Mithimna-Petra route described in Walk 7.

From Vafios village centre take the street downhill to join the Mithimna-Argenos road at the childrens' playground on the right. Follow the road downhill past the Taverna Vafios and continue as it
bends left and right in front of Taverna Ilias (ΤΑΒΕΡΝΑ Ο ΗΛΙΑΣ). In about 100 yards, on the left-hand edge of the road surface, look for a painted blue arrow to Petra (in English) pointing diagonally off to the left.

Follow in the direction of the arrow, then continue down the valley looking for the blobs of blue paint on rocks alongside the path to mark the way. For most of the route the path is unmistakable; there are the occasional unmarked decision points, but in these cases there is invariably a mark within about ten to twenty yards: if you don't come across one by then, go back and try the other option.

Most of the way is fairly open, although the path is steep in places. Towards the bottom it becomes narrow and can be overgrown with holly-oak and other thorny vegetation; unless you have leather legs long trousers are advisable.

When the path joins the Mithimna-Petra track (40 mins) turn right for Mithimna via the reservoir (Walk 7 in reverse, 45 mins) or left for Petra (Walk 7, 35 mins).

Walk 11
Vafios to Stipsi round the Mountain
Walking time 1½ hours

*Once you have walked to Vafios you will of course want to go on.
This continuation leads up and around the end of the Lepetymnos
range before descending into Stipsi on the southern face of the
mountain. From Stipsi return by taxi, or if you are still feeling
energetic continue walking and return via Petri (Walk 16 in
reverse). Alternatively make a diversion before reaching Stipsi
and visit Ypsilometopo (Υψηλομέτωπο). As you enter the village
you will see signs on the right to an ancient Christian basilica
nearby, but first you will probably be waylaid by the village priest,
Father Ignatius, who will take you to visit the parish church of the
Taxiarchs (Ταξιάρχες - Archangels). This beautiful church, with its
ornately gilded screen, lies by the roadside, but is almost hidden in
a wood of pine and fruit trees. You will also visit Father Ignatius'
herb garden, planted round the church, and come away with the
gift of a highly aromatic bunch of mixed herbs. (The basilica,
about ¾ mile south of the village, is early byzantine, dating from
the 6th century AD, but is now incorporated in the modern chapel
of Agios Dimitrios, built in 1954).
From Ypsilometopo retrace your steps to Stipsi, or take the village
taxi.*

In the village square of Vafios, facing uphill towards the Turkish
fountain and cafenions, take the street leading uphill to the right,
and follow it as it then leads downhill out of the village. Ignore a
tempting blue way mark arrow pointing up stone steps to a
footpath on the left.

The street becomes a concrete road bending right around
the end of the valley with a trekking trail sign on a tree to
the left at the apex of the bend. Follow the road as it leads
uphill and becomes a dirt track. There are views right across
Vafios to Mithimna until the track comes to the end of the ridge
and bends left (15 mins) to give vistas over Petra, Anaxos,
Lafionas and across to (yet another) Profitis Ilias to the north of
Scalachori.

Continue up the left-hand side of a wooded valley with walled and
gated orchards and olive groves on the right. After twenty-five
minutes there is an entrance off to the right through a steel gate

set in concrete
posts with a dry
stone wall on the
left. Walk 12
joins here.

After another five
minutes the track
reaches the head
of the valley and
hairpins right,
leaving a locked
gate and track to the left. Continue on the main track and at the
next left-hand hairpin continue to the left, ignoring the gated track
leading straight ahead. Carry on upwards past modern farm
buildings on the left and water troughs on the right, again ignoring
the track on the left before the buildings which leads down to
terraced orchards and animal sheds, and the one on the right
beyond the water troughs heading further uphill.

After fifteen minutes the track arrives at a whitewashed stone
circle on the left housing an open-air chapel. Behind it is a new
chapel, incomplete in 2002, with the dedication ΔΑΠΑΝΗΜΑΙΡΗΣ Ε
ΜΩΥΣΗ 1998. At about 460m (1500ft) this is the highest point of the
walk; from here it is downhill all the way to Stipsi, and behind the
chapel is a walnut tree where, provided you haven't already
emptied your water-bottle, you can celebrate with a drink in the
shade.

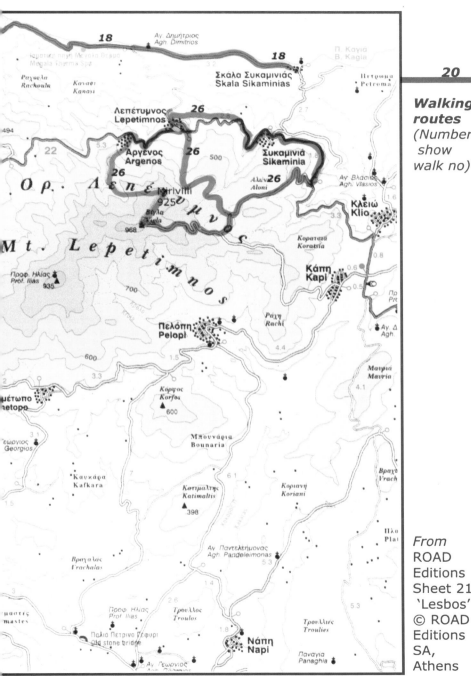

20

Walking routes
(Numbers show walk no)

From
ROAD
Editions
Sheet 212
'Lesbos'
© ROAD
Editions
SA,
Athens

Continue to follow the track as it descends through fields. Stipsi is one of the centres of the Lesvos honey industry, and you will pass beehives as well as pasture and arable land. Ahead there are views over central Lesvos down to the salt-pans of the Gulf of Kalloni, and Stipsi itself comes in to view on the hillside below.

Another fifteen minutes brings you to the road from Stipsi to Ypsilometopo, opposite a pine tree with a large new white house on the right. Turn left here to continue to Ypsilometopo (about thirty minutes) or right, and immediately right again, past the sports ground on the left, into the centre of Stipsi (10 mins). There are shops, cafenions, and a drinking fountain in the main square (dated 1992, and donated according to the inscription by the Stipsian Association of Athens - ΔΩΡΕΑ ΣΥΛΛΟΓΟΥ ΣΤΥΨΙΑΝΟΝ ΑΘΗΝΑΣ), but this is still very much a traditional Greek country town where everything, apart from the cafenions, closes in the afternoon. If you want to explore, much of the town lies on the side of the mountain below the main street: in fact the slope is so steep that the car park on the main street opposite the bus stop is built on the flat roof of the olive factory below.

As the road leads out of Stipsi towards its junction with the Petra-Kalloni road there is a rocky outcrop on the left crowned by the chapel of St George (Αγ Γεώργιος), with its bell hanging under a bright blue canopy. The chapel is normally closed, but its terraces give panoramic views over Stipsi and the Lepetymnos range, across the central plain to Kalloni, and to the west to the hills of Klapados, scene of the final battle between the Greek and Turkish armies in 1912 which ended the 450-year Turkish occupation of the island. (There were Turkish settlements around Klapados to which the Turkish army withdrew after being expelled from Mitilene) To reach the chapel, take the concrete path to the left of the school (ΔΗΜΟΤΙΚΟ ΣΧΟΛΕΙΟ ΣΤΥΨΗΣ) and continue between the white marker stones through the pine-wood to the steps leading up to it.

Then decide whether to continue home via Petri (Walk 16) or return to the village for a drink, a meal, and a taxi.

Walk 12
Through the Valley of the Mills to Vafios or Stipsi

Walking time approximately 3 hours from Mithimna, 2¾ hours from Petra.

The river gorge running down from the Lepetymnos mountains to the bay of Petra is lined with the massive ruins of old water-mills set amid spectacular volcanic rock formations. This is a strenuous but rewarding walk, parts of which are very overgrown, and includes thirty minutes in a rocky stream-bed through forest. Strong shoes and a hat to protect your head from overhanging branches are recommended.

Follow Walk 7 as far as the junction immediately above the double ponds (about 40 minutes from Mithimna, 30 from Petra). Take the gated track - straight ahead coming from Mithimna, to the right from Petra. (Not the track through the blue gate, which leads into an abandoned quarry and then quickly peters out).

After a few yards pass a long water trough on the left and continue along the track, with the Petra plain below to the right, through a second gate.

In ten minutes the track forks at a small chapel. Follow the main, left hand, track, through another gate, and uphill through an olive grove as the river gorge deepens on the right. After a further five minutes the track

acquires a concrete surface and begins to climb more steeply to yet another gate; the masonry of the first ruined mill appears on the right.

The track levels out and becomes grass-covered. There is a second mill on the left (5 mins). A short distance ahead, near a modern concrete weir and sluices, the track ends at an almost impenetrable barrier of stone, barbed wire, and thorny brushwood.

To continue up the valley, climb up the hillside to the right of the mill wall (there is a faint path leading up from the terracing between the first two olive trees) At the top of the wall go through a small gate and turn right on to a narrow path/ stream bed, with an orchard to the left. There is a steel water-pipe, partially encased in concrete, running along the side of the path, which soon opens out to a concrete cistern (10 mins).

Continue to follow the path along the open hillside above the ravine and the masonry of further mills. It is very faint in some places, paved in others, but runs parallel to the concrete-encased pipeline, and, in places, the original stone channels which fed water to the mills. After about fifteen minutes the hillside begins to become wooded.

The level path ends at another mill and turns sharp left uphill on to a narrow kalderimi through dense woodland. This part of the route is steep and <u>very</u> overgrown, and it is sometimes necessary to bend double in places to get through the tunnel of undergrowth and overhanging branches.

In ten minutes the path emerges on to a small grassy plateau above a massive mill structure to the right. At the entrance to the path is a post with a faded way mark, ⊙ and on a rock to the right is another mark: ⤶Petri   (By spring 2002 these marks had become almost   invisible, but there is funding for a local project to preserve the mills and restore this path, so hopefully they will shortly be renewed)

Walk 15 joins at this point, and to take it back to Petri or Petra follow the arrow to the path leading down to the stream. Otherwise continue along the path ahead for five minutes as it leads along the edge of the gorge with the stream on the right, following blue way marks, and past a water trough under a large old tree.

The way-marks continue to another water-valve. Look for a rock ahead with a sign in blue paint (in English!):-

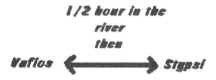

The path continues to follow the left-hand bank of the stream past more water installations including a small concrete hut. (If you are following this walk in the reverse direction, look out for this on the way downstream as an indication of the beginning of the path)

When the path ends continue up the stream-bed: a certain amount of scrambling and rudimentary rock climbing is required, and about five minutes before the end of this stretch there is a brushwood barrier dividing two properties which runs across the whole valley and has to be climbed over. Finally you will see an animal shed and stock pens ahead. Go to the left on to a track which leads up to a metal gate between concrete posts with a dry stone wall on the right (30 mins).

Go through the gate and you are on the Vafios-Stipsi track. Turn left and follow Walk 11 (in reverse) for forty-five minutes to return to Vafios, or right to continue to Stipsi, also forty-five minutes away (Walk 11).

Walk 13
Mithimna to Petri
Walking time 1¾ hours.

The tiny village of Petri nestles on the north-western end of the Lepetymnos range 260m (850ft) above the sea at Petra. The first known record of the village dates from 1602, when it was a mixed settlement of Greek and Turkish families, which it remained until the expulsion of the Turkish population between 1912 and 1923. (In 1909, of 60 households, 10 were Turkish). Today there are one or two holiday apartments, and a taverna, famous for the views of the sunset from its terrace, which is popular with both locals and visitors, but otherwise little seems to have changed. Despite the recently improved dirt road that connects it to Petra, seen from many angles it appears completely inaccessible.

From Mithimna take Walk 7 for forty minutes to the top of the double ponds. Instead of following the track as it drops down to the right between the ponds, continue on to the gated track ahead, ignoring the gate on the left leading into a small quarry. (Coming from Petra follow Walk 7 in reverse and turn right above the ponds) After about 200 yards pass a long water trough on the left, and in five minutes go through a second gate.

After another five minutes the track divides at a small chapel (this is where Walk 12 diverges). Take the grassy right-hand track, downhill, across a riverbed, and up, bearing right past a ruined stone building on the bank to the left (5 mins).

After a few yards a gate on the left leads on to a grassy track running uphill. (A kalderimi continues ahead and in ten minutes joins the dirt road from Petra to the St Constantine crossing - see below)

Take the left-hand, grassy track and follow it as it climbs, at first gently and then more steeply, with Petra harbour visible below on the right, through olives, oaks and gradually denser woodland. After leading through three gates, the track levels out into open scrubland, and then passes through a fourth gate to lead gently downhill to a junction with three other tracks (20 mins).

Ahead and to the left is a high volcanic outcrop on the summit of which is a shrine to St Constantine (Αγ Κωνσταντίνος), apparently

built on the site of an ancient watchtower of the Classical or Hellenistic period (ie c0-500BC). Take the concrete- surfaced road leading steeply uphill around the foot of the outcrop, with Petri visible to the right on the mountainside opposite. It levels out briefly, then swings right and climbs very steeply again past cattle-sheds on the right.

After twenty minutes, as the main track swings left to cross a ridge, another joins from the right. Take this, and follow it along the face of the mountain for fifteen minutes until it enters Petri village. Continue on the main paved street through the top of the village as far as the post box, then turn right down to the Petri Taverna a few yards on the left.

To visit the church, or return to Petra by Walk 14, continue past the taverna, and down the stone steps at the bottom of the street. To continue to Stipsi by Walk 16, carry on along the paved street past the post box, and down the dirt road to the first junction. Alternatively relax on the taverna balcony with food and drink before deciding where to go next.

The St Constantine (Αγ Κωνσταντίνος) Crossways

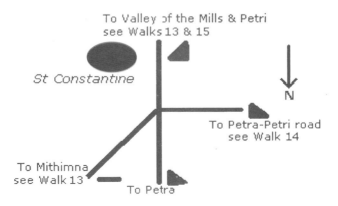

To Valley of the Mills & Petri
see Walks 13 & 15

St Constantine

N

To Petra-Petri road
see Walk 14

To Mithimna
see Walk 13

To Petra

Walk 14
Petra to Petri
Walking time 65 minutes

This is an alternative route to the hill-village of Petri, where the terrace of its taverna makes an ideal place for lunch or refreshments. The walk starts in the centre of Petra; however if you are coming from Mithimna by Walks 6 or 7 and do not wish to stop in Petra, you can cut off the corner by following the shortcuts described in those walks.

From the sea front square by the bus stop take the shopping street to the right (ΟΔΟΣ ΕΡΜΟΥ) running parallel to the beach road behind the Petra Womens' Co-operative guest house and taverna (there is a small local ouzo distillery in this street which is sometimes open to visitors), then turn left into Odos Sapfous (ΟΔΟΣ ΣΑΠΦΟΥΣ - Sappho Street) - past the Vareltzidaina mansion and continue under the rock of Panagia Glykofilousia. Where the street bears right by the 'Regular Market' and becomes Odos Nikis (ΝΙΚΙΣ - Victory) follow it as it leads out of town to meet the Petra-Kalloni road (15 mins).

Cross the main road and take the side road sign-posted to Petri (Πετρί) to the right of 'The Grand Café'. At first the road is level and straight, leading through fields, but after five minutes swings right and begins to climb. At this point follow the track which leads straight ahead, and when, after about 100 yards, it bears left into a field, keep right on the smaller track leading uphill. This deteriorates into a walled footpath between fields, and for about two hundred yards is also a stream bed.

Continue on the path as it winds uphill past a water cistern on the right (15 mins) then sharp left past a gate and railings. Go through the ruins of an abandoned Turkish village, named Chiliopigada, and cross a rock escarpment to rejoin a faint path between a rock face on the left and a fenced olive grove on the right. Follow along the fence, (at one point there is a small rock face to scramble up) with Petri facing you on the hillside ahead, to meet a dirt road by a stunted oak tree (10 mins).

Turn right on to the road, (for an alternative route to Petri from this point see Walk 15) and descend round a right-hand bend to rejoin the Petra-Petri road. Turn left and follow the road as it zigzags uphill passing the entrance to a rubbish tip on the right. Immediately after this there is a sharp left-hand bend and then, at the next right-hand bend a track leads off to the left of a new wall (10 mins). Follow this along the hillside to a new apartment block, then sharp right uphill past more new houses .

The track becomes a rough path leading on uphill to Petri church nestling under a cliff to the right. (If the church gate is open, go into the courtyard and to the left to see the spring flowing under the church) Follow the church wall to the right and take the paved and staircased street up into the village. Petri Taverna is towards the top of this street on the right (10 mins).

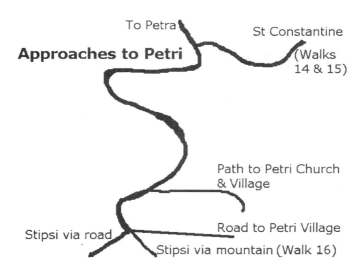

Walk 15
Petra to the Valley of the Mills or Petri
Walking time 1 hour 20 minutes to the Valley of the Mills or 1¼ hours to Petri.

This walk, as well as providing an alternative route to Petri, leads to the midpoint of the Valley of the Mills, so can be combined with Walk 12 to make a circular walk from Petra, or to continue through to Vafios or Stipsi.

Follow Walk 14 to the point where it joins the dirt road by the stunted oak tree. Turn left on to the road and follow it up to the St Constantine (Αγ Κωνσταντίνος) cross-roads (see page 35 for details) at the brow of the hill.

Turn right up the steep concrete road leading round the foot of the large volcanic outcrop to the left, on the summit of which is the

shrine to St Constantine (Αγ Κωνσταντίνος), Petri village is visible to the right on the hillside opposite. The road levels briefly, then swings right and climbs steeply again past cattle-sheds on the right (15 mins).   Petra is directly behind, the view bisected by the outcrop with the church of Panagia Glykofilousia to the left and the harbour to the right.

After a further five minute climb a broad track joins from the right. There is a large water-trough just above the junction, and a way-post with a small trekking trail sign (part of the 'Olive Paths of Lesvos ' scheme) pointing along this track.

For Petri follow this track along the side of the mountain for fifteen minutes. To reach Petri Taverna or the church, when you enter the village take the main paved track as far the post box, then turn down right. The taverna is a few yards on the left; the church is at the foot of the stone steps at the bottom of the street.

Otherwise, to continue to the Valley of the Mills, follow the track to the left over the ridge and downhill along the side of the valley. It goes through a gate and passes through oak trees with Mithimna and the reservoir visible in the distance to the left, then rounds the end of the valley and comes to another gate. Deep in the gorge to the left are the ruins of one of the water-mills. Beyond the gate the track becomes a path leading down into trees and across a stream-bed (15 mins).

Having crossed the stream climb diagonally left on a faint path up to, and on to the top of, a low wall (part of the massive masonry of another ruined water-mill on your left), by an old water-valve in the path. (Take care not to trip over this; if you have come out of the sun it can be quite difficult to see) Continue to climb for a few more yards, up and on to a rock marked with a faded blue arrow pointing round to the right. There is a small level grassy area here. If you turn to face the valley you will see in front of you a rock with a very faint way mark, just visible as Petri , and to the right, above the mill wall, a post way marked . This is the junction with Walk 12; to return downstream towards Petra follow the overgrown path to the right of the way mark: for Vafios or Stipsi take the path running upstream to your left.

Walk 16
Petri to Stipsi
Walking time 1 hour (plus an optional 50 minutes for the diversion to the summit of Mt Stipsi/Rousa)

This route climbs round the end of the mountain range behind Petri, with views across the valley towards Lafionas. For those who have an urge to get to the top of things, there is a diversion to the top of the mountain (known variously as Mt Stipsi, or Rousa (Ρούσσα) depending on the map), with, on the way, an 'aerial' panoramic view of the north Lesvos coast from Cape Petinos to Eftalou and beyond.

From the Petri Taverna walk up the street to the T-junction and turn right. Follow the street, and then the dirt road, downhill to the first junction (10 mins). (There is a diagram of this junction on page 37).

Turn sharp left uphill on to a gated track. This bends left, then right, heading south. After five minutes a minor track comes in from the left; ignore this. In another ten minutes the main track bends right as a second track leads temptingly off to the left through an oak plantation. Resist the temptation, and that of two minor tracks plunging down to the right a few minutes later, but stay on the main track as it continues to climb south along the edge of the valley, with Lafionas visible on the opposite hillside.

About thirty-five minutes from the start the track bends left round the end of the ridge. The Stipsi road appears below on the right: on the left a track runs off uphill to the left of a white barn, cistern and water-trough.

To reach the summit take this track, and follow it back round the side of the mountain as it climbs high above Petri and the plain of Petra. After twenty minutes it ends at a transmission mast. Continue up the path, through a gated animal pen, with a stable on the right. A short scramble up dry-stone terracing from here will bring you to a flat area of tree-planted meadow which is the peak (582m, 1909ft). Return by the same route to the junction by the barn.

To continue to Stipsi continue along the track, parallel to the road below. It leads through a farm, and after ten minutes reaches a junction. Here:-

Either take the right-hand track which runs downhill for five minutes to join the road via a short, steep stretch of concrete on the outskirts of the village. The Stipsi boundary sign is at this point, and also an old blue sign, in Greek and English:

←   Km 4
            ΠΡΟΣ ΔΙΑΣΤΑΥΡΩΣΙΝ ΠΕΤΡΑΣ-ΚΑΛΛΟΝΗΣ
            TO CROSSING PETRA-KALLONI

Turn left to walk into the village. After a few yards there is a new (1993) drinking fountain on the left. On the right a little further on is the school, and on a rocky mound in a pine wood behind is the chapel of St George (Αγ Γεώργιος).

Alternatively go uphill on the left-hand track and bear right, ignoring a track off to the left. The track runs along the side of the hill and after ten minutes the houses of Stipsi appear below. There are several side tracks leading off downhill, any of which will eventually lead down to the main street.

Walk 17
Mithimna to the Hot Springs of Eftalou and back
Walking time 2¾ hours

This walk takes you along the cliff tops and beaches to Mithimna's neighbouring resort of Eftalou and its medicinal hot springs. Return inland by a different route, or if you wish continue with Walk 18 along the shore to the picturesque harbour of Skala Sikamineas. The outward route to Eftalou takes 1½ hours, the return 1 hour 10 minutes.
The outward route is a little difficult in a couple of places owing to fences crossing the path and continuing into the sea. Be prepared to get your feet wet.

From the donkey station take the road uphill towards the castle, and where it forks above the cemetery, go right. Continue down the road until, after twenty minutes, it ends at the Aphrodite Hotel.

Alternatively, start from the castle, and follow the road downhill for about two hundred yards. Turn left on to the track opposite the pine wood leading to the Pansion Acropol, and then almost immediately right on to the track leading downhill, and follow it until it joins the road on a right-hand bend shortly before the Aphrodite.

At the Aphrodite the road continues as a track. Follow it as it leads round the right-hand boundary of the hotel, then turns right uphill past a new house and left again. Continue to the end of the track, with the hotel swimming pool and beach below to the left. Pass a large new walled development on the right. When the track ends turn right along the boundary wall of the property, then continue along the path to

the field wall ahead. Follow the path left along the line of the wall to the cliff edge, with the solar powered lighthouse to your left. Near the cliff large stones in the wall form a stile; cross the wall and continue down to a bay and beach (10 mins).

At the far end of the beach go over or round the end of the fence and resume the path up over the hill ahead. As it rises the path bends right to follow the line of the coast and Eftalou appears ahead on the left.

Continue on this path until it appears to drop down to the left along the face of the cliff (10 mins). Follow it down with care. At the bottom descend on to the rocks and walk along on the sea side of the fence to reach the beach.

Walk along the narrow beach for ten minutes, crossing a small stream-bed, until it ends at rocks and a path leads up to the road opposite the ΠΑΝΣΕΛΗΝΟΣ (Panselinos) apartments. Turn left and walk along the road past a fisherman's shack with its own tiny one-boat stone harbour and a narrow beach. The road rises to run behind a headland at the end of the bay past a track leading up into the hills on the right, with a 'No Hunting' (ΑΠΑΓΟΡΕΥΕΤΕ ΤΟ ΚΥΝΗΓΙ) sign marking the boundary of the nature reserve.

(This track leads up through a narrow valley for twenty-five minutes to end at a farm hut. A footpath continues for another twenty-five minutes and finally ends at a hut in an olive grove near a ridge. There is nowhere to go from here but back the way you came, but if you are staying in Eftalou, and want a fairly gentle morning walk, the wild flowers, particularly in spring, and the views, make this a worthwhile expedition).

Stay on the road over the brow of the hill as it drops down again towards the beach. Directly ahead at the far end of the beach the white dome of the thermal baths is visible. Rejoin the beach opposite the Hotel Molivos II and continue to the end, then go back on to the road as it swings uphill to the right.

After a few yards a paved track to the baths, which were restored and reopened in the early 1990s, leads off to the left. Follow the path under the cliff behind the modern building which houses administration and treatment rooms and through a doorway into a small tiled lobby. The bath, dimly lit through the ventilation holes in the domed roof, and full of steam from the naturally hot water (43-46°C), is through a low grilled entrance to the left (25 mins).

Exit on to the beach through the door to the right of the grille and walk along to the taverna perched on the cliff-face overlooking the next bay (5 mins).

Continue to Skala Sikamineas by Walk 18. To return to Mithimna climb the steps through the taverna and take the steep concrete driveway up to the road. Turn right and follow the road back down to the beach. Retrace the outward route back by the beach, along the road over the headland, and back along the narrow stretch of beach until about 100 yards from the end (about 40 mins).

Turn left off the beach on a track (there is a sign here to the Restaurant Tsipouri). A short distance up the track there is an old Turkish water fountain on the left, followed by the entrance to the Hotel Elpis on the right. When the track forks after this, go right past the entrance to the Restaurant Tsipouri (This area is called Tsipouri. Tsipouro is a drink similar to raki, distilled in the home from vine stems, figs, or mulberries, so possibly there were orchards here) Continue uphill through fields, and pass the rear entrance of the Pension Taverna Orpheus (ΟΡΦΕΑΣ) on the left.

The track continues to the right of the aqueduct tower. Turn right at the next junction (20 mins) along the dirt road past the Taverna Perikles. Rejoin the road leading up from the Aphrodite Hotel, turn left on to the castle road and follow it down to the donkey station (10 mins). Alternatively turn left at the junction before Taverna Perikles and immediately right to follow the path in the final paragraph of Walk 3.

Walk 18
Eftalou to Skala Sikamineas
Walking time 2 hours

This continuation of Walk 16 takes about another two hours, making Mithimna to Skala Sikamineas an ideal morning's walk. Apart from the taverna by the thermal baths at Eftalou, there are two more along the way, and plenty of opportunities to pause for a refreshing swim. Arrive at Skala Sikamineas in time to explore the village and have lunch at one of the harbour-side tavernas, then return to Mithimna by boat late in the afternoon. (There is a daily excursion boat during the holiday season, and one-way tickets are available from the travel office at the Seahorse Hotel on Mithimna harbour). Note that some maps and signs shorten Sikaminea (Συκαμινέα) to Sikamia (Συκαμιά); the place is the same.

From the taverna near the thermal baths you can continue along the beach to the headland at the far end, and then through a series of small bays under the cliffs. This involves a certain amount of easy scrambling over rocks between each bay - you may get your feet wet; note also that the bays are secluded and therefore predominately naturist. The cliffs eventually give way to meadows sloping up to the dirt road which here drops back down to the shoreline having led over and behind the headland. A track leads up to join the road at this point, but if you prefer a path continues along the beach, around the next low headland, and finally rises up to meet the road towards the end of the next bay, about thirty-five minutes after leaving the taverna.

Alternatively, climb the steps through the taverna and up its entrance drive to the road. Turn left on to the dirt road and climb round the head of the valley and on as it leads over the headland and downhill to the right and then, after about thirty minutes, left back towards the sea past a small country taverna (ΗΜΙΘΕΟΣ).

(This area attracts large flocks of migratory bird-watchers in spring, recognisable as they flit to and fro along the cliffs by their small white hire-cars and impracticably long lenses)

The road bends right to run parallel with the sea and passes the head of the track running down to the beach. Continue on the road as it continues along the coast, sometimes at sea level with

fields and olive-groves on the right stretching back to the foothills of the Lepetymnos range, sometimes rising through woodland over rocky headlands. From time to time tracks head off the road towards the hills; ignore these. There is a tiny beach taverna, which doubles as a fisherman's cottage, after forty-five minutes, immediately before a concrete road (doubling for a few yards as a riverbed) leads away into the hills, the new village of Lepetymnos, and the Sikaminea - Argenos road. Carry on along the shore and pass a small chapel (St Dimitrios - Αγ Δημήτριος) as the road starts to rise again.

Finally, after another forty minutes, pass a collection of millstones at the roadside on the left and the Medusa restaurant-bar (ΜΕΔΟΥΣΑ) perched on a rock to the right. The road becomes surfaced and five minutes later leads into Skala Sikamineas harbour, with the harbour church of Our Lady of the Fishermen (Παναγία των Ψαράδων), better known as the Mermaid Madonna (Παναγία της Γοργόνα), so named, it is said, from a wall painting of

the Virgin Mary with a mermaid's tail. (The picture no longer exists, if it ever did; there is a cynical view that the story was invented by the famous local author Stratis Myrivilis for his novel of the same name set here).

The harbour is lined with fish tavernas which at weekends are favourite destinations for Greek family parties, and there is no better place to relax with a beer and a meal while waiting for the boat back to Mithimna.

However, if you are still feeling energetic, the steep road out of the village climbs two miles to join the road from Mantamados that runs along the mountainside through Argenos and Vafios to Mithimna. Rising above the junction, in an easily defensible position against raiders from the sea, is the traditional hill-village of Sikaminea.

Walks 19 - 21
Petra to Lafionas

As you come over the ridge from the direction of Kalloni and head down through the hairpin bends towards Petra and the sea below, facing you on the hillside across the valley is the village of Lafionas (Λαφιώνας). Over 200m (650') above the sea, the village stands on a bluff looking down to the coast over two valleys, in a perfect defensive position against pirates, Turks, and tourists alike.

The following three routes give alternative walks to Lafionas (and back) from Petra, ending conveniently next to the local taverna. Once at Lafionas you may wish to continue on Walk 22 to Agios Alexandros, but be aware that buses come up here rarely, usually only in early morning and mid-afternoon in term-time to ferry local pupils to and from the secondary schools in Kalloni.

Walk 19
Walking time about 1¼ hours

From the sea front square take the shopping street (Ermou - ΟΔΟΣ ΕΡΜΟΥ) leading off to the right behind the Petra Womens' Co-operative guesthouse, and then the second street on the left (Sappho - ΟΔΟΣ ΣΑΠΦΟΥΣ) Pass the Vareltzidaina mansion on the left (or go in for a free visit and guided tour) and continue up the street around the foot of the rock on which stands the church of Panagia Glykophiloussa (Παναγίας της Γλυκοφιλόυσας)

As the street bends right to the junction by the 'Regular Market' mini-market take the paved street off to the right and walk along about 50m to the next junction, where a concrete lane leads ahead. Turn left here on to the paved street (sign posted ΚΑΛΛΟΝΙ). Where another paved street comes in from the left continue ahead on a dirt road alongside a watercourse on the left until about twenty minutes from the start you reach the new 'Petra bypass' road.

Cross the road and take the track directly opposite. Walk between olive groves for about ten minutes until you come to a Petra council depot on your left - a wire compound with assorted vehicles belonging to ΔΗΜΟΣ ΠΕΤΡΑΣ. Almost immediately turn on to a track leading off to the right (continuing ahead leads quickly on to the main Petra-Kalloni road) Five minutes later cross a concrete bridge over a stream and begin to climb gently. Lafionas comes into view ahead and above to your right. In another five minutes follow the track as it bends right, ignoring another leading off to the left (Walk 20 takes this alternative)

You now begin to climb more steeply. Follow the main track as it bends round to the left, ignoring a smaller path leading down into the valley on the right.
Petra is now comes into view down to your left, with Petri directly ahead across the valley. Then swing right and continue climbing with a valley falling away to your right. Pass a set of steel gates on the left and climb a section of concrete-

surfaced track up to the entrance to farm buildings. (A concrete surface on an otherwise unmade track is a sure sign that even the Greeks think it's steep). Lafionas is now visible dead ahead.

Fifteen minutes after the start of the climb the track comes to a T-junction, where there is a painted way mark ●● on a rock to the right. (Walk 21 joins here) Turn left and walk gently downhill; the track first becomes concrete and then paved as it arrives at the edge of the village. It climbs up under a terrace built out from a house overhead and comes to another T-junction.

Turn left here past the cafenion on the corner (for those who have seen Lance Chilton's 1997 booklet, 'Walks in North Lesvos', this is Jimmy's Café, though it has no sign, and indeed I have yet to find it open) Follow the street round to the right past a church on the left with a shrine and water fountain in the outside wall. Then pass another cafenion on the left to reach a railed terrace at the end of the winding road that leads up from the main road in the valley below. Here there are seats overlooking the valley, post box, telephone and bus shelter, with a new (1998) drinking fountain in front. Up steps on the opposite side of the square is the restaurant TO ΑΙΘΡΙΟΝ ('Clear Sky') with a terrace where you can admire the view back over the route you have just come while enjoying more substantial refreshment.

Walk 20
Walking time about 1 hour

Follow route 19 for the first thirty-five minutes as far as the track coming in from the left.

This time turn left here and follow the track uphill for about five minutes, then turn right on to a recently bulldozed track. (Parts of this track have been washed away by storms and are very rough).

Climb steeply through olive groves for about fifteen minutes. (Ignore a smaller track running off to the right into the valley after about ten minutes). As it approaches Lafionas the track runs between stone walls and then narrows to become a short kalderimi up to a paved street.

Turn left immediately and follow the street round to the restaurant TO AIΘPION and the square/terrace at the entrance to the village

Walk 21
Walking time about 1½ hours

This third track to Lafionas winds up between the two conical hills that form punctuation marks between the sea and the end of the Skotino (Σκοτεινό) range on the side of which Lafionas sits.

The track leads off the bypass road (which until 1999 was itself a track) near its Anaxos end. To reach it from Petra you can take the sea front road towards Anaxos, follow it as it bends left uphill away from the sea, and at the junction near the top of the hill turn left again on to the new road. However this part of the Petra sea front is narrow, busy (in spite of the bypass, which is hardly used), and has an unprotected drop into the sea on one side, so can make for uncomfortable walking. An alternative is to start as for Walks 19 & 20, but after turning right at the 'Regular Market' continue straight ahead instead of making the next left turn. This lane leads parallel with the coast through orchards and market gardens until it passes a small chapel on the left and rises on a short stretch of concrete to rejoin the main road. Turn left and climb a few yards up to the junction with the bypass.

Turn left on to the bypass and walk down it for about five minutes to a steep concrete track that leads diagonally off to the right (this is the second track to the right after the junction). Climb up this track: it bends round to the right with a cottage on the left at the corner, and shortly afterwards passes white iron gates leading into an olive grove on the right.

Carry on climbing; as it winds upwards there are views down to Anaxos, the sea, across to Cape Petinos and beyond, and back to Petra and Mithimna (don't forget to look behind from time to time).

After climbing for about twenty minutes the track bends left high above the coast, with the bay of Anaxos below to the right, and heads inland.

It begins to descend and then swings left around the head of a valley, with a large rock outcrop on the right-hand apex of the bend. Climb again over the brow of the hill and drop down to join Walk 19 at the way marked (●●) junction below Lafionas.

Walk 22
Lafionas around Roudi to Agios Alexandros
Walking time about 1½ hours

The small mountain (c450m, 1500') which rises behind Lafionas is called Roudi (Ρούδι). On a grassy plateau on its western flank overlooking Skoutaros, surrounded by pine forest and rocky outcrops, are the remains of the early Byzantine (c4th century AD) monastery of St Alexander (Αγ Αλέξανδρος) - medieval Greek monks, like their brothers elsewhere, clearly had keen eyes for desirable locations which would not have disgraced a modern estate agent. In the 17th century the site was occupied by Turkish colonists who used the stones of the monastery to build their own settlement and mosque. In 1954 the remains of the monastery were discovered and a small chapel was built on the site. There have been further sporadic excavations since, and some of the remains, an early altar, and carved pediments and capitals from the monastery church, are now housed in the chapel.

A track above Lafionas roughly follows the contour the whole way around the mountain, except for an uphill stretch towards the end, making this a pleasant circular extension of a walk from Petra or Anaxos. (There are picnic tables and a small shelter for a refreshment break at the monastery)

From the square in Lafionas take the street on the left going into the village, follow it as it bends round to the right and then continue uphill past the next junction to a T-junction with an old whitewashed fountain in the wall facing you. Turn left and climb steeply up to the next T-junction, (there is a rusty sign on an electricity pole here - ΠΡΟΣ ΑΓΙΟΝ ΑΛΕΞΑΝΔΡΟΝ ->) and then go right up a stretch of concrete. This leads to the left of a house and becomes a narrow kalderimi, with the bay of Petra visible down on the right. Where the path forks keep to the right and then follow it left up through the trees. Look for a way mark ••<--> on a rock to the left of the path. Fifteen minutes from the start there is a large rock on the right with a way mark •. Follow the kalderimi to the right and continue with the valley on your right, occasionally passing further way marks ••.

After another five minutes the path comes out past a stone hut and water trough on the right on to a small open plateau. Follow the short track that leads up diagonally to the left to join the main track running along the side of the mountain.

Turn right on to this track and follow it with the plain of Petra, and later Anaxos, far below to the right. After about twenty minutes, shortly after a rough track leads off down to a rubbish tip on the right, cross a small ridge and Skoutaros comes into view across the wide valley ahead. The track bends down to the left, and in another five minutes arrives at the fenced and gated enclosure of Agios Alexandros on the right. There is a new drinking fountain (probably still unconnected) on the left of the track here, and a somewhat superfluous way mark •• on a rock just inside the gate.

From the monastery the track climbs back into the forest and continues round the mountain with wooded valleys falling steeply away to the right. It climbs into more open terrain and after about 25 minutes comes to a ridge where there is a seat and another fountain, this one connected and working. You are now back above Lafionas, facing east, with Petri to the left, and Stipsi ahead, visible across the valley.

At the junction ahead turn left downhill to return to Lafionas. (The track ahead leads through the abandoned Turkish village of Klapados, site of the final battle to liberate Lesvos in 1912, and then on to join the Petra-Kalloni road - see Walk 23) Follow down past a large water cistern and trough on the left. At the next fork go right down a steep concrete road, past another cistern on the right, to a car-park above the village. Go down right again and immediately left into the top of the village. The concrete road becomes a paved street. Turn right at the T-junction, left at the next, and then right again into ΟΔΟΣ ΠΙΤΤΑΚΟΥ. Follow this down to 'Jimmy's' cafenion (see Walks 19 & 21) and from there return to the square or continue to Petra.

Walk 23
A Forest Walk to Klapados and Lafionas
Walking time about 1 hour 50 minutes

This walk follows a forest trail along the hillside overlooking the central valley of Lesvos, passing through the ruined village of Klapados, site of the final battle between the Greek and Turkish armies in 1912 which liberated Lesvos from 450 years of Turkish rule.
The easiest way to reach the start of the walk is to take the Mithimna - Mitilene service bus. After crossing the ridge at the end of the Lepetymnos range behind Petra, the road drops down past the junction for Stipsi. About 4 km beyond this junction there is a filling station on the left. One kilometre further on the road swings right through forest before beginning its descent to the plain of Kalloni. At this point there is a forest road off to the left, and immediately afterwards another rising sharply to the right with a picnic 'pavilion' at the junction. Ask to be put down here.
(If you have the ROAD Editions map there is a measuring point at this spot. The map reference is approximately 12°20'E 15°30'N. See also the map in the centre pages)

Walk up the track past the picnic pavilion. There is a sign at the beginning designating this an 'ecological route', and there are benches and occasional picnic tables at particularly scenic points along the way. After climbing for about fifteen minutes, with views to the right across the valley towards Stipsi, the track levels out and branches, with a subsidiary running off downhill to the right towards the road below. It then continues uphill again, heading approximately west.

After another ten minutes the track reaches a crest, with views down to the left to the Gulf of Kalloni. Ignore the track that branches off downhill in that direction, and continue on the main track as it climbs round to the right back into the forest, with a walled orchard and stone hut on the right.

In five minutes you reach a level grassy area on the left with picnic tables. Go on uphill past a water cistern on the next right-hand bend and continue to climb gently northwards. Ignore the rough track leading diagonally off uphill to the left after another ten minutes; just beyond here there is a bench on the right at a viewpoint looking across the valley towards Stipsi, Pelopi, and the Lepetymnos mountains. This is more or less the highest point of the walk, and a good place for a rest to admire the view.

The track now begins to descend. After another five minutes it bends left at another seat and continues downhill, with the ruins of Klapados visible on the hillside ahead. As you approach the track bends to the right and leads along the foot of the village. Near a sign on the left commemorating the battle there are the domed remains of the village bathhouse, by a spring which now feeds a new water-trough. Above it is a giant plane tree, still alive despite having been almost destroyed by fire.

Carry on up out of the village past another hexagonal pavilion above the track on the left, and curve left to head west on the level again. Pass another seat on the right and, after five minutes, a cistern on the left. Follow the track round to the right and up again, ignoring a track down to the left and two leading uphill on the right.

In five minutes pass another seat and start to descend again, with Petra, Mithimna Castle, and the Turkish coast visible through the trees ahead. Carry on for fifteen minutes, then cross a cattle grid, continue down to a right-hand hairpin bend by yet another pavilion, picnic table, and a water fountain dated 1998. This is quickly followed by a left-hand hairpin, and a right-hand bend leading over a concrete bridge and across the head of a valley, until in another fifteen minutes you reach the junction above Lafionas. (There is another 'Ecological Route' sign here).

Turn right and follow down past a large water cistern and trough on the left. At the next fork *(a sign here, for those coming up the hill, points right for both Ag Alexandros and Klapados. If you are walking this route in the reverse direction, ignore this and go left)* go right down a steep concrete road, past another cistern on the right, to a car-park above the village. Go down right again and immediately left into the top of the village. The concrete road becomes a paved street. Turn right at the T-junction, left at the next, and then right again into ΟΔΟΣ ΠΙΤΤΑΚΟΥ. Follow this down to 'Jimmy's' cafenion (see Walks 19 & 21) and from there return to the square (fifteen minutes) or continue to Petra.

Walk 24
Petra to Anaxos
Walking time about 1 hour

It is difficult to avoid the main road from Petra to Anaxos, but it can become a bore to walk, especially if you are doing it regularly during a two-week holiday. In particular, the sea-front stretch from Petra square, with coaches squeezing past and a sheer drop into the sea on one side, can induce an acute sense of insecurity.

Here is a much more pleasant route, though as the final stage involves a scramble over rocks it is not suitable for late night returns from the taverna in the dark.

Start as if walking to Lafionas by Walk 21, but instead of turning left on to the Petra - Anaxos road and climbing to join the bypass road, turn right and walk down towards the sea.

As the road swings right back to Petra turn left on to the track along the shore under the cliff. (There is a 'No entry' sign at the beginning of this track, and also a large sign marking the beginning of the Petra - Lapsarna Trekking Trail). Walk along the track (recently extended, it soon narrows into a footpath) for about ten minutes, past a couple of beach-side tavernas and a tiny harbour. The island of St George (Νησί Αγ. Γεώργιος) aka Rabbit Island and its smaller companions are offshore to the right.

In another five minutes the path disappears. Carry on along the rocky shoreline for a further five minutes to the next headland, where there are more moorings for small boats, and a gated track leading off the beach (the gate is normally locked, with a sign in English 'Private Road - Do not Pass')

At the next small headland, another five minutes on, either follow the small path up and over the rocks, or get your feet wet paddling round (the steps up the cliff to the left lead to a group of private cliff top chalets) and you are on Anaxos beach, with its waiting tavernas and sunbeds.

Walk 25
Anaxos to Ambelia Circular Walk
Walking time outward about 45 minutes, return about 1 hour.

If you have become slightly jaded with the disciplined sunbeds and massed bars and tavernas of Petra and Anaxos, try Ambelia. The shallow bay keeps the sea calm and warm (even by Greek standards), and the beach is clean and underpopulated (and naturist-friendly), with one small taverna/bar and a river-mouth full of terrapins.

Walk along Anaxos beach, or along the road behind the beach, for fifteen minutes, towards the far south-west end. (The road swings briefly away from the beach, then bends right to cross a riverbed by a concrete bridge) Pass the last fish taverna on the beach, then turn left alongside a block of beach studios onto the last track before the end of the beach. When the track ends continue on the path bearing right through gardens and olive groves to a T-junction. Turn right and follow the path between cottages.

After ten minutes you will pass a low white cottage lying below the path and a kalderimi leading off on the left. After another white cottage on the right, the path ends at a gate. Go through the gate and follow the footpath diagonally left across the field towards the cliff top. From here the path follows the cliff top about fifty feet above the sea. *(In a strong wind, or if you suffer from vertigo, take extra care along this stretch. However it may be reassuring that the locals do ride their donkeys along here at a canter)*

The cliff path climbs between walls, passes through a gate and continues along a short steep rocky stretch. It levels out and then begins to descend round the head of a tiny cove with an isolated chapel built above the beach.

After about fifteen minutes drop down towards the beach, go through another gate and follow the path on to the beach. (If you are returning to Petra in this direction, go round left where the path forks just above the beach - do not continue on the path to the right alongside the wall).

To return to Anaxos walk to the far end of the beach and take the concrete road

that leads steeply away to the left, marked by a small trekking trail sign. After fifteen minutes come to a T-junction. The road to the right leads to Skoutaros; turn left and in thirty minutes the road undulates its way back through the hills and across the river (more terrapins) to join the Anaxos - Skoutaros road. Turn left along the road and in ten minutes reach the centre of Anaxos.

Walk 26
Chalikos and Vigla Circular
Walking time to top of Vigla 2¼ hours. Return **a** 2½ hours **b** 2¼ hours.

This is a full day's walk, fairly strenuous in parts, taking in the ruined village of Chalikos and the forested slopes of the Lepetimnos range, before climbing (almost) to the highest point in northern Lesvos. To reach the starting point from Mithimna or Petra you need a car or taxi; these instructions assume the former. Take the Vafios road out of Mithimna and continue from Vafios past Argenos: down on the left on a level plateau you will see the new village of Lepetimnos, rather incongruously looking more like a German or possibly American suburb than a Greek village. It was built to accommodate the inhabitants of Chalikos after their village was largely destroyed and abandoned after a landslide about forty years ago. Continue to the road junction signposted to Lepetimnos and drive down into the village to park.

There is constant argument as to whether Vigla or Olympos, the imposing white mountain in the south of the island near Agiasos, is the higher - both are officially 968m (3176'). However the top 20m or so of Vigla is fenced off to protect a military communications post on the summit, and is rarely accessible. To stand on the highest point in Lesvos you will therefore probably have to go to Olympos - it is possible to drive all the way to the top!

From the new village walk back up the road to the junction with the main road and turn right. In another two minutes pass the old schoolhouse of the ruined village balanced precariously above the road with its steps ending in mid-air and its sign - ΔΥΜΩΤΙΚΟΝ ΣΧΟΛΕΙΟΝ ΧΑΛΙΚΟΣ 1936 - still engraved above the door. A few metres further on take the concrete ramp leading up diagonally on the left, which soon gives way to a wide kalderimi.

Follow this up through the ruins of the old village to a T-junction where there is an old fountain in the wall ahead. Turn left here and continue round the edge of the village to another T (5 mins).

Go left up three steps on to a narrow kalderimi and continue to the left through a gate. In a few metres there is an old trekking trail marker (a yellow triangle with a white centre) on a tree to the left.

Follow the path for ten minutes as it climbs between walls and across a narrow concrete water channel, then through woodland. There is another short stretch of kalderimi as the path rejoins the water channel, and then in five minutes crosses the stream and climbs a steep bank.

Follow the path up the bank, and where it divides a few metres later go right. It levels out and on the right there is a large tree with a rather belated way mark ← ✝

Continue along the path in the direction of the arrow. Pass a group of three giant hollow trees on the right, and continue ahead as a small path comes in from the left. A stream-bed briefly joins the path, before the path diverges up to the right, then crosses the stream again between a group of four more large hollow trees and leads up to the right round the highest of the group (15 mins).

Cross the stream once more and follow the path up to the left and then right alongside a stone wall and chain link fence. Go through a gap in a brushwood fence and pass a ruined stone animal pen and another two giant hollow trees. Opposite the second tree the path turns sharp left uphill and then zigzags right and left to lead to an old, but still constantly flowing, Turkish water fountain (dated ١٥٤١ 1241AH, 1826AD)and water troughs (10 mins), a good place to stop for refreshment.

The path now continues uphill to the left. It bends right and left and climbs alongside a wall, leaving a small hurdle gate to the left. Cross a small open area and climb up over bulldozer spoil to join the end of a track (5 mins). (*NB This track was extended between 2001 and 2002: if it is continued further this section of the route may change*)

Continue along the track with Lepetimnos village and the sea
visible below on the left. In five minutes go through a gate and
continue along the wide grassy track. After another five minutes
tracks come in from the right (barred by iron gates) and left.

Continue ahead on the
main track as it begins
to run gently downhill,
then bends right to
wind round the head
of a deep valley and
climb again to another
gate. Down on the
left you can see
the roofs of Sikaminea
and Skala Sikamineas.
In fifteen minutes
come to a T-junction with another broad track. (* see return route
a below)

Turn right. Almost immediately the track bends sharp left and
leads between private fenced and gated groves. After five minutes
another track forks off downhill to the left (leading to Kapi). Stay
on the main track as it bends up right round the end of a ridge.
The television masts on the summit of Mirivilli are mow dead
ahead, with the summit of Vigla further to the left.

The track continues to wind uphill; after fifteen minutes a
right-hand hairpin encloses two circular cattle pens and a large
water trough. Go on uphill for another thirty minutes until a track
drops away to the right to cross the saddle to Mirivilli. Continue
round to the left and climb for another five minutes: the track ends
at the gate in the fence enclosing the summit of Vigla. If it is open
another five minutes will take you to the top, but remember that
you are now in army territory.

To return there are two options:

a. via Sikaminea

(If you did not drive to Lepetimnos and are thinking of returning by the excursion boat from Skala Sikamineas take this route)

Retrace your route down the mountain for forty-five minutes as far as the junction (*). Instead of turning left carry straight on over a small rise, and then along the wide level track with a stone wall on the right.

After fifteen minutes the track swings left and begins to wind downhill, with Kleio and the Sikaminea - Mandamados road below to the right. In ten minutes cross a cattle grid, and in another five another, and emerge on to the Sikaminea - Mandamados road by a sign to ΠΥΡΟΦΥΛΑΚΕΙΟ ΒΙΓΛΑΣ (Summit of Vigla).

Turn left and walk along the road for twenty minutes (1.8km) to reach the beginning of Sikaminea at the junction of the road leading down to Skala Sikamineas. If you are heading for the boat turn right here and follow the road down three kilometres of steep hairpins to the harbour (allow an hour). Otherwise, to explore the unspoilt hill village take the ramp up to the left, or continue along the main road (there is another ramp up into the village after about two hundred metres, opposite a roadside taverna).

To return to Lepetimnos carry on along the main road as it follows the edge of the valley. It bends sharp right after about five minutes and passes a small chapel and fountain in a shaded courtyard on the left. After another five minutes there is a large 'Sikaminea - Kapi Trekking Trail' sign on the right. From here it is about 1½km on the road to Lepetimnos.

However if you are still feeling energetic and ready to get off the road take the small footpath running diagonally down to the right just before the sign. In five minutes turn right where another path joins from the left, go down, and almost immediately go left at the next T.

Follow the path along, with a wall on the left. A stretch of kalderimi climbs briefly, then descends on steps. Go down through woodland with a wall on the right, to the bottom of a valley and a stream, then continue on the level on a soft path, with a view of the sea down on the right (10 mins).

The path leads back into trees and descends again. It bends round to the right and climbs on kalderimi. Bear left at a gate and climb steeply over a brow and down again with a wall on the right to reach an open area (5 mins). There is a steep drop into an olive grove, with Skala Sikamineas behind you to the right.

Two minutes further on go left by a gate, on to a wider and better defined path, which becomes grassy along the edge of terracing. Follow it back into woodland and bend right. In five minutes the path bends left with the entrance to an olive grove down on the right.

Continue up on to kalderimi and climb in the open with the sea away on the right and an olive grove behind a chain link fence on the left. Go left into the olive grove and towards the corner, then right under the trees, back on to the path and follow it round to the left (8 mins). Go along the path as it reverts to kalderimi leading down and across a stream, then bending right under a high stone wall on the other side. It finally bends left and climbs twenty metres to join a dirt road by a small trekking trail sign.

Turn left on to the road (right leads down to the coastal track from Eftalou to Skala Sikamineas) and walk uphill for five minutes (a concrete surface begins after a few metres) until it bends round to the right. There is a large rock on the left-hand side of the bend: immediately before it turn left up stone steps leading to a path. Follow this for five minutes; it leads along the edge of a valley and then turns left under the wall of the churchyard to come out in Lepetimnos village by the church gate.

b. via Argenos

Come down from the summit of Vigla past the first right-hand hairpin, and then go sharp left down the partly concrete track across the saddle to the television masts on Mirivilli. Go to the left of the masts and look along the line of the power cables coming across the valley to supply the transmitters. The cables run across to a ridge, and then towards the end of a track near another, smaller mast. In turn that track runs down behind the far hill to the village of Argenos, which is visible below to the right.

From the transmitters follow down to the first electricity pole, and then to the left of the power lines, higher up the valley, across to the far ridge. There is no path (except random sheep tracks) across this stretch, which is steep, loose scree. Take it slowly and carefully, and make sure each foothold is firm before trusting your  weight on it. Do not try to hurry - from the transmitters to the top of the track can take an hour. Once you reach the ridge, cross it and continue along near the top; although rocky, the going is now firm and relatively easy - there is a path further down the hillside but it is not worth the effort of scrambling down to it. When you come to group of ruined stone animal pens go back over the ridge and join the end of the track.

Follow it downhill for twenty-five minutes until it reaches Argenos sports ground (ΑΘΛΗΤΙΚΟ ΣΤΑΔΙΟ ΑΡΓΕΝΟΥ) with a small cemetery beyond. The track becomes a concrete road and forks. Take the right fork and follow the road into the village. At the T-junction at the end, turn left and right, then right again in a small square in front of a marble fountain. Turn right again to reach the village square and taverna in ten minutes.

Walk down the paved village street past the taverna on the right and village school on the left. (Ignore the trekking trail sign at the end of the footpath just below the taverna - at one time it led back to Chalikos and Lepetimnos, but since the construction of the main road in 1996 no longer goes anywhere). The street becomes concrete and in five minutes leads down to the main road.

Turn right on to the main road and walk downhill for ten minutes to the spring of the Archangels (ΤΑΞΙΑΡΧΗΣ) on the right. (On the left of the road there are the remains of an old water mill fed by the spring).

In another two or three minutes the first ruins of Chalikos come into view above the road to the right, and shortly afterwards a trekking trail sign 🚶 About twenty metres before the sign leave the road on the 🚶 left (to the left of a chain link fence and the right of the concrete retaining wall of the road). Go back under the wall and pick up a path leading down to the right. It bends right under a stone retaining wall then left on to kalderimi steps covered with loose stone. Continue down, cross a water gully, turn right and reach the road on the edge of Lepetimnos village. Turn left into the village to return to your car (15 mins).

Some Circular Walks

Here are some suggestions for combining walks to make circular routes. The list is by no means exhaustive; if you have by now read the walk descriptions and looked at the sketch map you will already have come up with some of your own. The timings are very approximate; an asterisk against a walk number means that only part of the route is used.

Mithimna - Petra - Mithimna (starting from Mithimna or Petra)
(Walks 6 - 7)   2¾ hours

Mithimna - Vafios - Mithimna
(Walks 8 - 10 - 7*)   3½ hours

Mithimna - Petri - Petra - Mithimna
(Walks 13 - 14 - 7)   4¼ hours

Mithimna - Vafios - Stipsi - Petri - Mithimna
(Walks 9 -11 - 16 - 13)   5¾ hours

Petra - Petri - Petra
(Walks 14 - 13* - 7*)   2¾ hours

Petra - Vafios - Petra
(Walks 15 - 12* - 11* - 10 - 7*)   4 hours

Petra - Stipsi - Petri - Petra
(Walks 12 - 11* - 16 - 14)   4¾ hours

Petra - Vafios - Mithimna - Petra
(Walks 7* - 10 - 8 - 6)   4¾ hours